The Complete Kitchen, Bathroom and Bedroom Planner

The Complete
KITCHEN, BATHROOM
and BEDROOM
Planner

Laurie Williamson

The Crowood Press

First published in 2001 by
The Crowood Press Ltd
Ramsbury, Marlborough
Wiltshire SN8 2HR

British Library Cataloguing-in-Publication Data
A catalogue record for this book is available from the British Library.

ISBN 1 86126 434 8

Typefaces used: Melior (text) and Helvetica (captions).

Typeset and designed by
D & N Publishing
Baydon, Marlborough, Wiltshire.

Printed and bound in Singapore by Craft Print International Ltd.

CONTENTS

INTRODUCTION

If you're planning a major purchase such as a new kitchen, bathroom or bedroom, you should have as much information as possible at your fingertips so that you can make the right decision. *The Complete Kitchen, Bathroom and Bedroom Planner* is packed full of information and sound advice to help you do just that.

In the majority of homes the kitchen is the social point and forms a vital support system for the household. It is not only a room for the preparation and eating of food but a room where the hubbub of everyday life turns smoothly and efficiently. The bathroom is also a focus of attention. With choices varying from the modern, contemporary look to a reproduction of traditional, period-style bathrooms it is often as carefully planned as the kitchen and, though practical during the day, in the evening can be as cosy and comfortable as the bedroom. And the beautiful bedroom, a true reflection of your taste and personality, will be as carefully planned and styled as any other area in the house. Some bedrooms will be planned for single-person occupancy and others to accommodate more than one person with an emphasis on en-suite facilities and dressing areas. Whichever room you are planning to improve *The Complete Kitchen, Bathroom and Bedroom Planner* with the unique 3D planner will help you visualize your dreams and guide you towards a successful and memorable outcome.

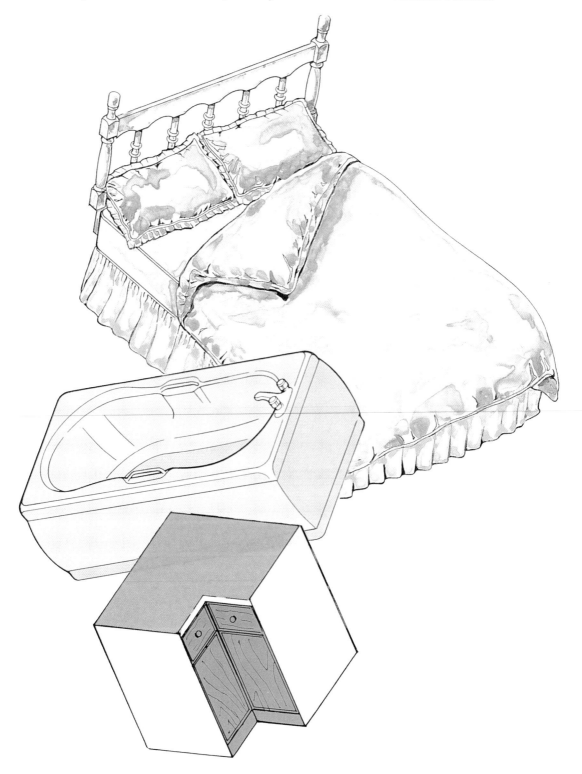

KITCHEN PLANNING

For many people the kitchen is likely to be the focal point of the modern home. It is often a room where families meet regularly and where the general everyday activities of the home unfold. A kitchen is an area where meals are prepared and food is stored and it may well be an area where meals are eaten and clothes are laundered. Whatever its functions, that may be many and varied, the kitchen area is important to the modern household and, for this reason, it needs to be planned meticulously.

Modern kitchens have for many years been the single most important selling point of a house. In fact, such are their importance, that kitchen planning and kitchen manufacturing have over recent years grown into an industry of huge proportions. New appliances such as dishwashers and microwaves have been introduced to assist in food preparation and such is their popularity that kitchen designers of new properties automatically include them in their calculations. In fact the art of kitchen planning has become so detailed that few of us believe that we have the knowledge or confidence to plan the kitchen ourselves, which accounts for the number of kitchen specialists about. For this reason alone, it is impossible to imagine how kitchens operated fifty years ago such is the progress that has been made.

Of course there should always be a good reason for changing your existing kitchen. It may be too small, the wrong shape or the wrong colour. Whatever the reason you must take care and plan the whole project properly. Look closely at the positions of existing doors and windows and any other major obstacles that are often insurmountable and that the kitchen will need to be designed around. Next, and of equal importance, look at the positioning of the services. Where is the drainage outlet located? The waste from the kitchen sink, dishwasher and even washing machine will need to be directed into the drainage system in the most effective and well-designed way. Existing electrical points and light fittings may need repositioning and water pipes introduced or diverted to provide water for sinks and other related accessories. All these things need to be considered because they are the structural points around which your new kitchen may well have to be designed.

After you have considered all the structural implications and before you make any decisions about the style of your new kitchen, or the colour, you must first decide how much money you are prepared to spend in total. Will this figure include kitchen planning? Will it include installation and any structural or decorating jobs that may be required before or after the kitchen is fitted? Is the figure you are considering relative to the resale value of your house? These are just general points but they are important and will have a direct bearing on the successful outcome of this project.

When all of these decisions have been made then you can look at planning the new layout yourself. A new, fully fitted kitchen should, of course, be planned by

The 'Provence' kitchen in natural ash, with green marble worktops.

(Top) Cooking is a pleasure in this superb 'Traditional' maple kitchen.

(Above) Eye-catching distinction with beech-style edgings and worktops.

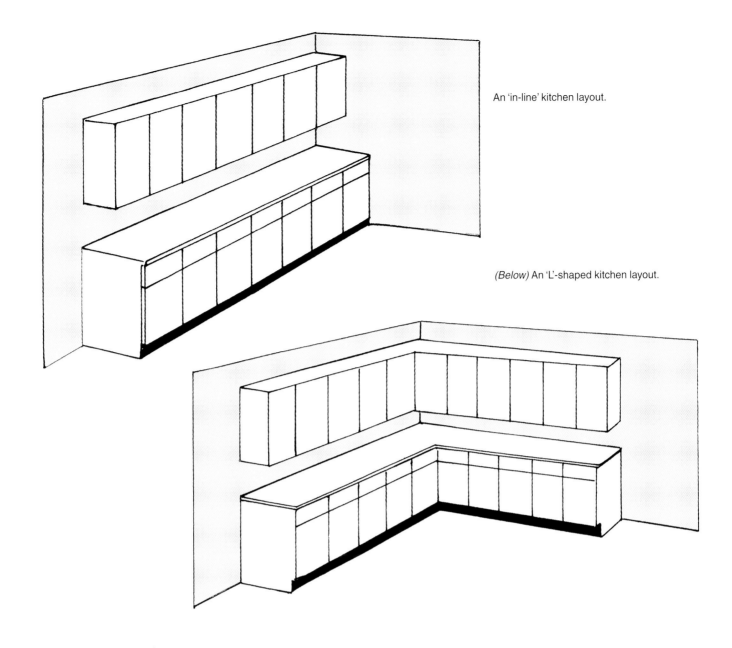

An 'in-line' kitchen layout.

(Below) An 'L'-shaped kitchen layout.

professionals but do take some time to consider exactly what you want the kitchen to do for you. You may, or may not, love to cook in which case there will be an emphasis on kitchen appliances and work surface areas whereas the reluctant cook may be happy with just the bare essentials. You may want to leave room for a dining table or you may just want to improve upon the style and colour of the kitchen you already have.

After these decisions have been made the next step is to call in the experts, provide them with a list of your requirements, and ask them to test your theories to see if they are practical. Many offer a complete service including the fitting of appliances and the final decorating work. What is important is that you fully understand what is and is not included in the price given. The units themselves may in fact only amount to a small proportion of the overall cost of the new kitchen so working from brochures alone can be extremely misleading. Armed with your own requirements and, hopefully, with not too many preconceived idea, choose your kitchen specialist carefully and arrange for a home visit. For this service there may be an initial charge but it is often refunded should you place your order with this company.

Selecting a kitchen specialist from the multitude available may look rather daunting at first but in fact, from your own planning ideas, and from demands placed upon your pocket the possibilities reduce rather dramatically. The cost of

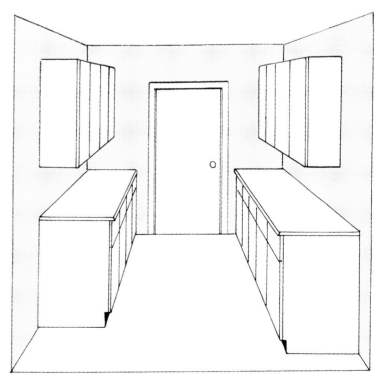

A 'galley' kitchen layout.

The beautifully styled 'Cook's Kitchen'.

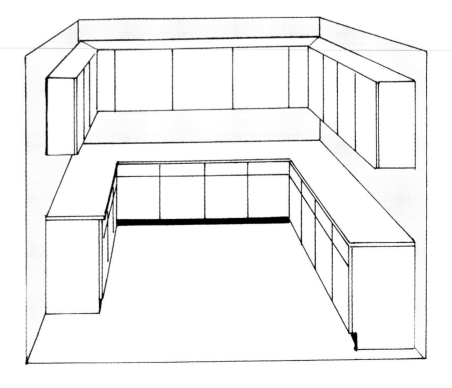

A 'U'-shaped kitchen layout.

self-assembly modular units will vary greatly from hand-crafted furniture produced to your own bespoke design and this alone will make the area of operation far simpler to work in.

LAYOUT

The first and most important point when planning a kitchen is the layout. What layout is best for you and best for your kitchen. There are three very important areas to consider from a working point of view and these are food storage, cooking appliances and washing-up facilities. The food storage area may include a fridge and a freezer as well as cupboard space for dry foods and tins. There may be room for vegetables to be stored and for cleaning equipment. The cooking facilities may include cooker, microwave and hob while the washing-up facilities could be a sink and a dishwasher. Whatever the function of the new kitchen the floor area must be used wisely to ensure that any activities to be carried out can be done in safety and comfort.

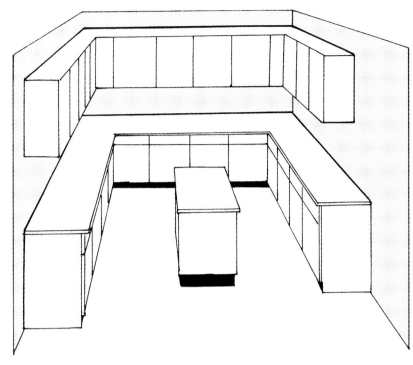

An 'island' kitchen layout with peninsular unit.

(Below) Draw up a visual guide before making irreversible decisions.

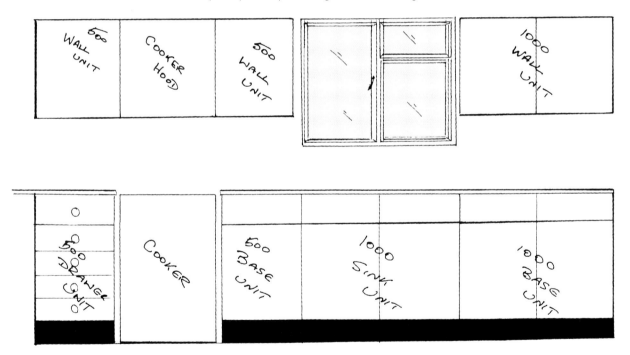

If the new kitchen is to include a dining area then access to and from the table should not, if at all possible, interrupt cooking activities. Accidents can easily happen when children and adults are allowed to wander aimlessly around when hot food is being prepared.

To prepare you own layout, before consulting the experts or working from ideas available, draw an outline of the area of the kitchen and cut out units you would like to be included in this area. If you think there is adequate room for a dining table measure the area required to use this facility properly and cut out a unit to size so that it can be placed in a position that will give you a good idea what space is or is not available. It is true that modern kitchens, indeed modern houses, are centres for space-saving ideas but the kitchen area must

be comfortable to work in so always allow extra room for any activities to be carried out in it.

MEASURING UP

What is possible will depend very much on the size of the room available. To produce a basic layout that will best fit your kitchen, first measure the floor area and transfer these measurements to a suitable grid sheet. Accurate measurements are extremely important when installing self-assembly or rigid kitchen units because their sizes are predetermined before manufacture. Always double check measurements before transferring them to the grid sheet and always use a *metric* measurement because modern kitchen units are built to metric sizes and this will greatly reduce the risk of mistakes. The wall measurements should be taken from two or three different positions to check how square the room is and it will provide an early warning about discrepancies before installation. If the walls are a long way out of square then alterations to the units and work surfaces may be required. Be sure to relay this information to your kitchen planner when you discuss your requirements in greater detail. Record these measurements on your grid sheet then add the position of doors and windows. Door positions are vital to the smooth running of a kitchen where interruptions to work areas should be kept to an absolute minimum. Window positions will determine where the main light and ventilation sources are.

The next measurements to add to your plan are drainage, plumbing and electrical point locations. If you are planning a major overhaul to the kitchen area then these services may need to be relocated and if not then your kitchen may be designed around them. What is important is that you are fully aware of their location before determining the positions of sinks and accessories.

As well as a floor layout plan you should make wall layout plans as well. For this you will require the window and door measurements and positions so that you can add the likely positions of wall and tall units. Standard metric measurements for all self-assembly and

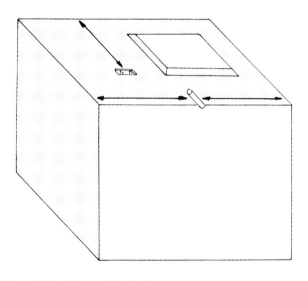

(Above) Check the position of existing drainage fittings.

(Below) The clean lines of this kitchen help to create a pleasing geometry.

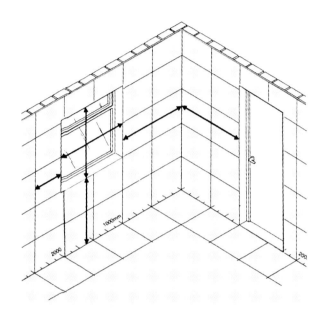

Measure distances between important points such as windows and doors.

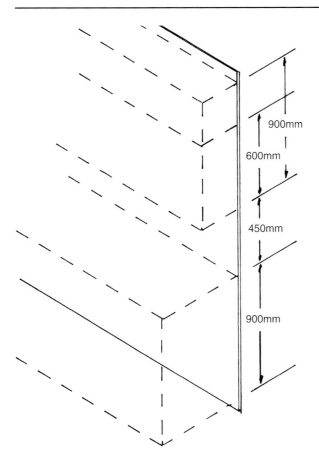

(Above) The approximate measurements to work from.

rigid units are provided in kitchen brochures so early selection and ideas are made easier. A measurement that seldom varies a great deal is the gap between the base unit and the wall units, which should be in the region of 450mm. This will provide enough room for the work surfaces to be used effectively.

And finally when you plan the kitchen layout you will have taken into consideration what function the kitchen plays in your household. You may entertain frequently or never and you may want the kitchen to be a social area or used simply for food storage and preparation. Whatever layout you choose the measurements you worked from will give you a good idea of what you may be able to achieve before you discuss your kitchen in greater detail with a qualified kitchen planner.

For hand-crafted units, built to personal requirements, initial measurements can be a little more casual. When firm decisions are required the units will be built to suit the space available and a professional kitchen planner will provide accurate plans for your consideration before the craftsman starts work.

SERVICES

Properly planned services in the kitchen will make for a safer and healthier environment. Any alterations to these services will be best carried out by a professional, but the availability of easy-to-use fittings and expert advice can assist the competent do-it-yourself enthusiast to carry out these projects successfully.

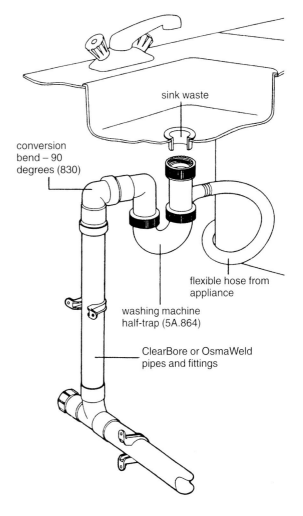

(Left) The inspirational 'Oak' style kitchen.
(Above) Fitting a sink waste using Osma fittings.

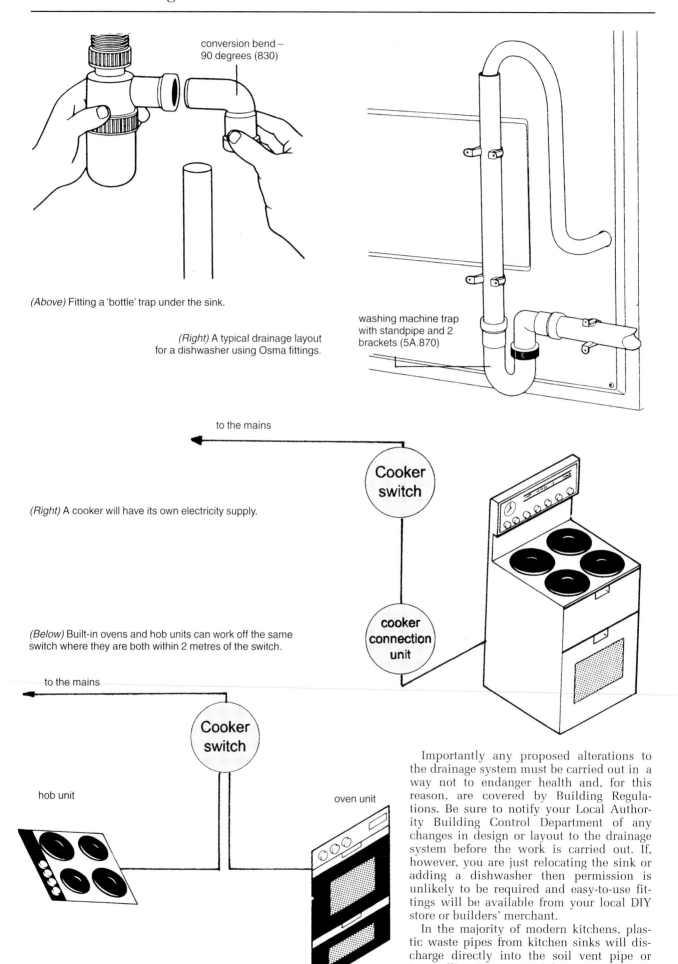

(Above) Fitting a 'bottle' trap under the sink.

conversion bend –
90 degrees (830)

(Right) A typical drainage layout
for a dishwasher using Osma fittings.

washing machine trap
with standpipe and 2
brackets (5A.870)

to the mains

Cooker
switch

(Right) A cooker will have its own electricity supply.

cooker
connection
unit

(Below) Built-in ovens and hob units can work off the same
switch where they are both within 2 metres of the switch.

to the mains

Cooker
switch

hob unit

oven unit

Importantly any proposed alterations to the drainage system must be carried out in a way not to endanger health and, for this reason, are covered by Building Regulations. Be sure to notify your Local Authority Building Control Department of any changes in design or layout to the drainage system before the work is carried out. If, however, you are just relocating the sink or adding a dishwasher then permission is unlikely to be required and easy-to-use fittings will be available from your local DIY store or builders' merchant.

In the majority of modern kitchens, plastic waste pipes from kitchen sinks will discharge directly into the soil vent pipe or into gullies. The required dimension of pipes and fittings for this purpose must be 40mm with the maximum pipe run being 3 metres long. When in position, waste pipes must then be secured to the wall by using the appropriate waste pipe clips.Under the sink a bottle trap will be attached to the sink plughole and it is designed to hold water that will provide a barrier to prevent gases and fumes entering the room from the drainage system. This bottle trap will also catch and store potentially blockage-making materials. Occasionally the bottom section of the bottle trap can be removed to allow for cleaning and the removal of blockage materials to prevent them from reaching the main system.

Traditionally the kitchen sink will be situated close to the kitchen window with the waste water discharging into an external gully. But today, with sinks sometimes being situated centrally on island units, the discharge of waste into the drainage system can be more complicated and, in these instances, the services of a professional plumber may be required.

PLUMBING

Cold water is brought into the kitchen via a service pipe connected to the rising main. At this point there should be a stopcock for shutting down the system in case of emergency or repair. The hot water to be supplied to the kitchen sink will come from the hot water cylinder and all the fittings will be in copper pipe of 15mm gauge. Hot and cold water connections may also be required for washing machines and dishwashers. These supplies can be teed off the existing plumbing system. For the do-it-yourself enthusiast flame-free plumbing fittings are available and these fittings are easy to install and incredibly reliable. However, unless you are extremely competent, it may be wise to employ the services of a reputable local plumber. Manufacturers of appliances will recommend the use of a professional for installation with the removal of guarantee cover should the appliance fail due to a DIY installation.

ELECTRICS

The kitchen of the modern home will have three electrical circuits, a ring circuit for lighting, a ring circuit of power points and a separate circuit for the cooker, each of which will be connected individually to the main consumer unit. The cooker is the largest consumer of electricity in the home and will require its own electrical circuit. It may be a single, free-standing cooker unit or it may be separate oven and hob units. Wiring for each appliance can be fed from the same electrical circuit, but their proximity to each other will determine how many and where the isolating switches are to be positioned.

The next set of electrical appliances to be considered will be the stationary appliances such as the fridge and the dishwasher. These will be connected to the ring main via a fused outlet or fused spur, always allowing one fused outlet per stationary appliance. Allow enough flex from the appliance to the socket to assist the replacement of, or cleaning behind them.

Finally, add at least six socket outlets, positioned just above the work surfaces, to cope with the smaller appliances such as kettles and mixers. Try to locate the sockets close to where the appliances are likely to be used and always install double socket units.

Adding to or amending any part of the electrical supply system in a kitchen will be a job for the professionals. Unless you are particularly confident with electricity it is advisable to recruit the services of a qualified electrician to carry out the work in this, the most potentially dangerous electrical operations room in the house.

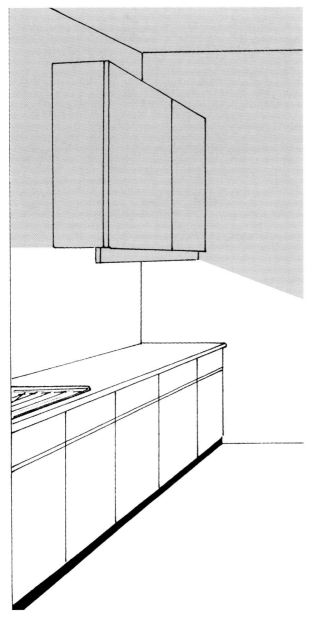

Concealed lighting can be very effective.

Concealed lighting can be both practical and extremely attractive.

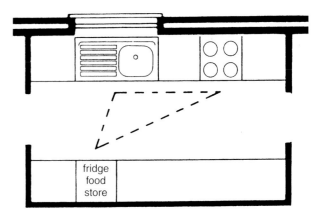

The work triangle in a 'galley' kitchen.

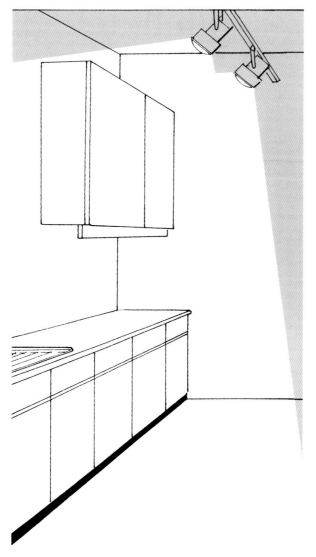

Well-positioned spotlights are very popular.

LIGHTING

Kitchen lighting should be both comfortable to work with and practical. There are a number of ways to introduce light into the kitchen where well-planned lighting can bring about a total transformation. New technology offers a variety of choices including downlighters, uplighters, backlighters and concealed lighters influencing different moods and different shades. And the lighting you choose will also have an effect on colour schemes, on wall tiling and on floor coverings. So it is important that you choose the lighting you require before any decisions are made on these other points. Some remedial work may be required, cutting holes in ceilings or chasing cables into walls for wall fittings or switches. And of course the position of the kitchen units will dictate where the lighting needs are greatest and where the work areas will attract the highest priority. But although simple overhead strip fluorescent tube lighting may provide all the light you require it may not in reality create the right mood or the right shade to complement your new kitchen.

The range of possibilities for lighting the kitchen is really quite extensive. Work surfaces can be lit from concealed strip lights positioned under wall units or they can be lit from spotlights recessed into the ceiling void. The cooker may well have its own light from a cooker hood while the kitchen sink can also be lit from spotlights. There may be a separate dining area, requiring lighting of its own, possibly directly over the dining table or maybe with the use of side-lights and table lamps to create the effect you desire. There is no right or wrong way to light a room, it is a matter of choice, but remember the kitchen area is best shadow free and the light colour you choose should have the right effect on the food you are preparing.

WORK TRIANGLES

It is important that you do not leave the layout of your new kitchen to chance. The end result needs to be both attractive to look at and effective to work in. For this reason the 'work triangle' is a good guide that can be used when you decide on the position of certain important items such as the kitchen sink and the cooker. Try to consider whether the layout you have will be easy to use and remember that there are three stages to the cooking process: preparation, storage and cooking. If you conveniently position these sections together then cooking should be more enjoyable and less tiresome.

When you look at the work triangles illustrated you can clearly see how this process works. The safest solution will be to situate the cooker or hob on the same unit run as the kitchen sink and where this is not possible to situate it close to the sink. The 'work triangle' should not be interrupted by tall units or by doors, bearing in mind that passing traffic through a kitchen can be extremely dangerous. The kitchen and more importantly your cooking space must be free from small children.

I have listed a few 'do's' and 'don'ts' to assist you when you plan your work triangle but the size and shape of your kitchen will finally determine what you can and cannot achieve.

DO'S
- Do allow at least 1200mm between units placed on opposite walls.
- Try to position the hob and the sink on the same unit run.
- Position the sink near a window to take advantage of natural light.
- Make sure larger electrical appliances have their own fused socket.
- Make sure there are sufficient power points for electrical gadgets.
- Make sure curtains and blinds are nowhere near hobs and ovens.
- Ensure there are always base units below wall units.
- Try to place an oven and hob in a well-ventilated position.

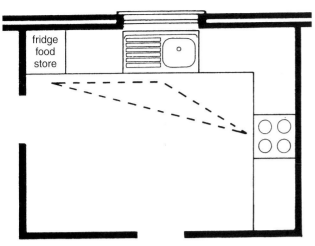

- Do leave at least 400mm work surface next to hobs and sinks for elbow room.
- Make sure there is somewhere safe for children to play where you can keep an eye on them.
- Try not to position a sink in a corner.
- To simplify plumbing arrangements, try to situate sinks, washing machines and dishwashers close to the drainage facilities.
- Make sure all services comply with Building Regulations and are installed by professionals.

DON'TS
- Do not interrupt the work triangle with doors.
- Do not place wall units above a table.
- Do not interrupt the work triangle with tall units.
- Do not position the hob or oven close to a door.
- Do not position power points close to sinks.

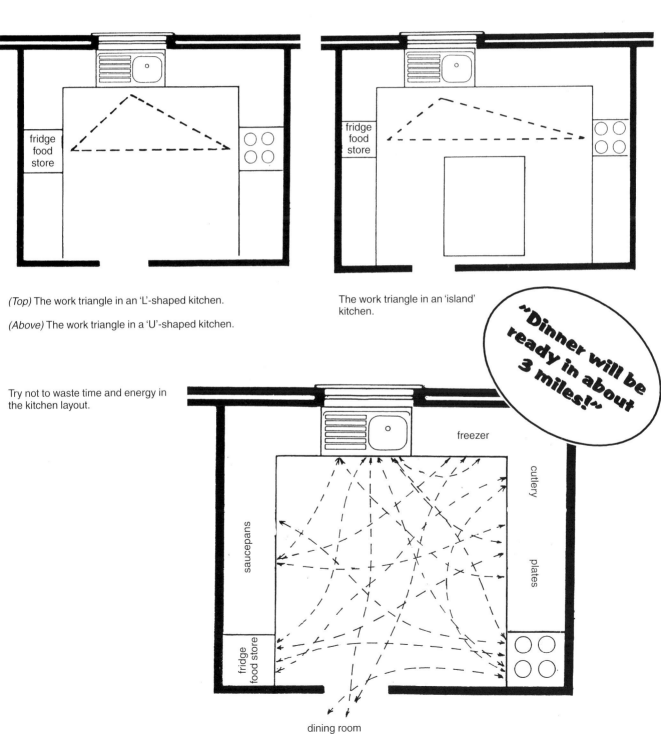

(Top) The work triangle in an 'L-shaped kitchen.

(Above) The work triangle in a 'U'-shaped kitchen.

The work triangle in an 'island' kitchen.

Try not to waste time and energy in the kitchen layout.

"Dinner will be ready in about 3 miles!"

freezer

cutlery

plates

saucepans

fridge food store

dining room

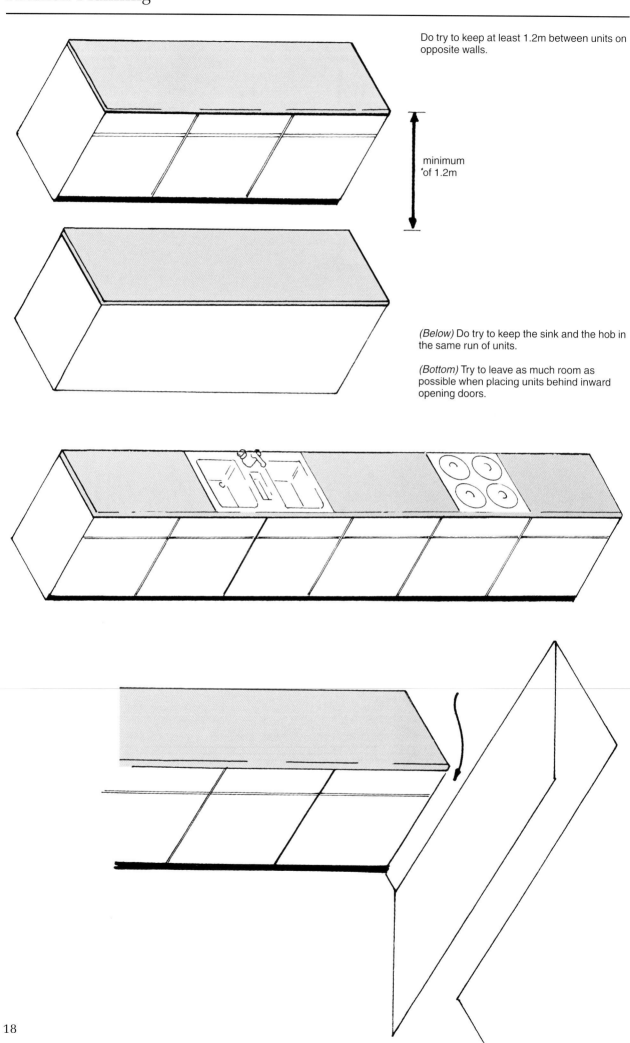

Do try to keep at least 1.2m between units on opposite walls.

minimum of 1.2m

(Below) Do try to keep the sink and the hob in the same run of units.

(Bottom) Try to leave as much room as possible when placing units behind inward opening doors.

Do not position units over open spaces or above a table.

(Below) Try not to interrupt the work triangle with doors.

(Bottom) Self-assembly modular units come in flat-pack form.

- Do not place a wall unit over a hob unless it is a cooker hood unit.
- Do not place sinks or hobs next to tall units.
- Do not allow passing foot traffic to interrupt the work triangle.
- Do not position a tall unit in the centre of a run of base units as it will interrupt the work surface area.

MAKING A CHOICE

For many people the kitchen is a reflection of the lifestyle of today's homeowner as they become more selective in their requirements. Standard modular flat pack and off-the-peg kitchens are still extremely popular and offer extensive choice while hand-made, craftsman-built kitchens, with overtones of fashionable country living, are quickly becoming an equally favoured option. Self-assembly and rigid kitchens tend to be of the modular type. A modular kitchen unit is one that is of a set size in height and depth and varying in standard widths, 300mm, 600mm, 1000mm and so on. It is the opposite of a custom-built kitchen where the units are built to fit a given space.

The self-assembly units are kitchens of the modular type, bought as a flat pack and assembled at home, that answer the call for immediacy while rigid units may take weeks before delivery and hand-built will take even longer. The ranges available include solid wood, wood and laminate and laminated fronts available in a huge range of colours. Larger do-it-yourself superstores stock off-the-peg units in every conceivable size and to meet almost every need. They offer in-house planning servic-es and a range of accessories and fittings to suit every need. And of course every kitchen is priced to suit. Fitting and assembly instructions are provided with every pack, making them as easy to assemble as possible. In fact all you need is a screwdriver, a spirit level and a kitchen.

(Above) Tall dresser units combine well to create attractive storage areas.

A modern version of the traditional farmhouse look.

(Below) The solid elm doors and drawer fronts are finished to a classic medium oak colour.

OPPOSITE PAGE
(Top) A solid oak kitchen washed in rich green.

(Bottom) Design simplicity and quality materials combine to produce kitchens built to last.

Rigid units are kitchens of the modular type that are assembled in the factory and delivered in boxes to the customer's home. These units tend to be more sturdy than self-assembly because the sides, back base and top of the units are assembled using wooden dowels and glue. They are then clamped in a jig to ensure they are perfectly square and rigid. The door fronts and drawer fronts are added at the factory and the complete unit is delivered ready for the installer to fit. As with the other modular kitchens, the range of styles and material finishes available is extremely extensive. It is not always easy to distinguish between self-assembly kitchens and rigid kitchens other than the fact that the latter, because the joints are glued, will not have plastic screw caps at the top and bottom of the unit sides hiding screw heads.

Made-to-measure, custom-built and hand-made kitchens represent the top end of the kitchen market. This does of course mean reaching deeper into pockets but you will be paying for craftsmanship and quality materials. The manufacturer will work closely with the customer and every unit will then be built to size and installed. With made-to-measure furniture there are few restrictions, and this does not only apply to the materials, it also applies to the cost. The highest price may not always be the best value so check each manufacturer thoroughly and visit their showrooms. Arrange for a home visit to discuss your requirements and be sure to discuss your budget.

SOLID WOOD

Kitchens made from solid wood are an eternal favourite. They are both aesthetically pleasing and built to last. Although expensive solid wooden doors mellow with age, and while the units may be scratched and wear with use, this only adds to their inherent beauty. Among the wide variety of woods available the most common are oak, ash and pine.

(Above) A well-designed kitchen can be the most popular room in the house.

Rigid modular units will be delivered already assembled and glued together.

(Right) Oak, the king of timbers, with well-oiled maple worktops combine in this 'Victorian' kitchen.

Kitchens made from oak, available in light, medium and dark finishes are traditionally English. The oak tree is synonymous with English heritage, steeped in history and has a timeless quality. Ash is a much lighter wood and is also common to the British Isles. It is generally well-grained and is becoming increasingly popular. Pine, softer than oak, is a lovely mellow honey colour, grown in colder climates while the hard mahogany is from warmer climates. Kitchen manufacturers who make made-to-measure units will have their own favourites for various reasons. Certain woods are suitable for specific purposes and provide the right effect in certain locations. Wood is not a natural reflector of light and, in some instances, may just be too dark for some kitchens. Discuss your requirements with the manufacturer and, because solid wood kitchens are generally more expensive, take time over your decision and look at all types of wood to see which suits you and your kitchen best.

Of course, solid wood kitchens can be a variety of colours. The wood can be oiled to complement the existing colour and enhance its life expectancy or it can be painted. Painted units are available in a multitude of colours to suit the purchaser with many kitchen manufacturers using a wide range of techniques to produce exactly the right finish for your kitchen.

WOOD VENEER

Wood veneer is a finish to doors and drawers that creates the same effect as real wood. It is often less expensive than real wood and it can be quite difficult to spot the difference. The veneer is bonded to a base material such as chipboard and is available in almost any wood colour and style. There are few drawbacks to buying a kitchen with wood veneer unit fronts; it may not have the timeless qualities of the real thing but it will be stable and the doors are unlikely to warp. Manufacturers of both self-assembly and rigid units offer a wide range of styles and colours in veneer and veneer panelled units. The units may have a painted or a laquered finish to provide an appearance similar to their contemporaries allowing the wood grain finish to show through.

LAMINATED

Laminate is a very popular choice for kitchens. It is durable, hard-wearing, easy to clean and relatively inexpensive. It is also available in a wide variety of colours and textures with gloss and matt finishes. There is one glaring problem with laminated finishes and that is uniformity of

A limed oak finish is both attractive and distinctive.

The 'Edwardian' kitchen in maple with oiled maple worktops.

The pale maple-effect colour can be inspirational.

(Above) A maple-style finish with unobtrusive design details.

(Left) Put freshness first.

(Below) The warmth of real wood has a contemporary touch.

(Top) A touch of Mexico with terracotta tones.

(Above) The dazzling white kitchen will delight any home.

A fashionable 'Shaker'-style kitchen.

colour. The kitchen units you see in the display show-room may not exactly replicate the units that arrive from the factory. So, when the units do arrive, first check the fronts for uniformity of colour and, if there is an odd one out seek to change it immediately. Another slight draw-back with the plastic laminate finish is that it will wear much more quickly than wood or wood veneer and will scratch more easily. Wooden kitchens age beautifully where laminated kitchens get old.

Before making your final choice, remember that whatever you choose will be with you for a long time. There is a vast array of kitchen styles and colours to consider and of course there is the cost. I have sought to compare the different types available and also to look at self-assembly, rigid or made-to-measure but the final decision will be yours. For many families the kitchen is the heart of the home and all of family life revolves around it so discuss your plans with all family members. Consider their ages and how long you intend to live there. Is your family increasing in size or growing up and moving away? Are you looking for a short-term improvement or a long-term investment? These are questions that need to be answered when you address this major change to the home. Of course there is a case for self-assembly units that can be quick to install where made-to-measure will take a great deal longer. And finally should you decide to move house a well-designed, well-fitted kitchen will always be a valu-able selling point.

QUALITY

'You only get what you pay for' is not really what you want to hear when your new kitchen starts to perform in ways you never believed possible. It is true that there are risks when buying off-the-shelf units cheaply but the risks are not always there to be considered. But con-sidered they must be. The majority of kitchen units are built from melamine-faced chipboard of varying thick-ness. Some are built in the factory as rigid units and some are flat-packed for self-assembly. The rigid units built in the factory are likely to be sturdier than flat pack units, generally, because the joints are first dowelled and then glued together in special jigs. Self-assembly units, on the other hand, are not usually glued together but fixed with special screw fittings. The melamine boards used will also vary in dimension from 15mm in thickness upwards. Make sure you are fully aware what the units are made from because shelves and wall units may well suffer when used to store heavier items. They may bow and lose their shape before collapsing alto-gether. Of course these units are perfectly suitable for kitchen use but care must be taken when storing heav-ier items such as crockery and glassware.

The problem with looking at kitchens in a showroom is to know what to look for, in short, what the profes-sionals would look for. You can try the drawers and you can open the odd door or two but generally the quality is not easy to spot – that is, the quality of the materials used and the fittings with which the units are held together. These are points a quality manufacturer will be proud of so ask the kitchen salesperson to explain to you why this kitchen is good enough quality for you, and then make sure you only pay for what you get.

(Right) Worktops to match your requirements in iroko, beech, maple and oak.

(Below right) Subtle lighting and the warmth of a hardwood worktop creates the right mood and atmosphere.

WORKTOPS

A well-chosen worktop can be the icing on the cake for a new kitchen. Available in a wide range of materials and a multitude of colours your choice must be both versatile and durable. If the worktop area in your kitchen is only small you may choose the opulence of marble or granite and if not then perhaps a tiled worktop or a laminate will be your choice. Whatever you finally choose you must remember that the worktop is often the most visible part of the kitchen and subject to the most punishment. It must be able to cope with everyday wear and tear, handle contact with hot and cold objects and still be easy to clean and hygienic. The vast majority of modern worktops are manufactured from high density wood particle board covered with a decorative laminate providing a high degree of durability. Worktops are easy to install, available in a variety of widths and lengths and offer a wide range of colours at very reasonable prices.

Hardwood worktops can be costly but are also extremely durable. They provide a certain warmth and character to a country-style kitchen. The woods used to make worktops include beech, iroko (African teak), oak, maple and pine. All hardwood tops must be treated with oils recommended for this purpose, that is all except the pine worktop.

(Below) Hardwood worktops can be a feature of any kitchen.

Reversible breadboard over bread drawer.

Built in knife slots at the back edge of this worktop.

Marble chopping boards or slate pastry boards can be set to finish flush with the surface.

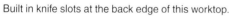

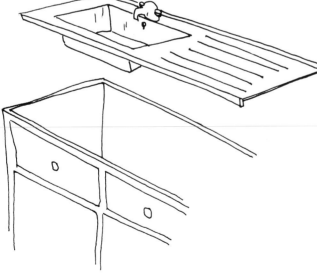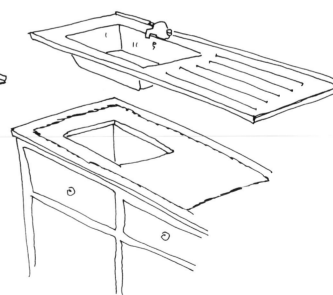

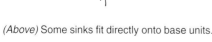

(Above) Some sinks fit directly onto base units.

(Right) Where a kitchen sink is fitted on a worktop be sure to seal the joints with mastic.

Pine worktops need to be sealed with a suitable laquer to provide a hard-wearing and protective finish. To prevent the worktop from staining during the first few weeks it should be oiled, according to manufacturer's instructions, and water must not be allowed to lie on its surface. Oak, in particular, can stain quite badly if water contact is not kept to an absolute minimum.

Worktops formed from marble and granite are heavy and solid, hard-wearing and versatile. Expensive and opulent, these materials provide a timeless elegance and quality that complements almost any environment.

Corian is a man-made material that can look like marble but is, in fact, a fusion of natural materials and clear acrylic. It is very durable and hygienic and resistant to most household stains. Available in a multitude of colours, Corian can be cut and joined to meet virtually any design requirement. And finally ceramic and mosaic tiles are also popular as a work surface with a wide range of patterns available that will complement almost every kitchen. This glazed surface is extremely durable and heat-resistant but extra care must be taken to avoid cracking and also when the surface is used for the preparation of food.

SINKS

For too long the kitchen sink has been synonymous with hard labour, but no-one would consider planning a new kitchen without giving extra attention to this vital implement. With at least 70 per cent of time reportedly spent at the kitchen sink, it is vital to make a good choice. The modern kitchen sink is good looking, functional and available in a wide range of styles. It can be inset, set into a hole cut in the worktop, or it can be seated on a base unit. Stainless steel sinks are the most popular, they are long-lasting and heat-resistant but they are liable to scratch and dent. Satin, linen or textured stainless steel is particularly desirable where scratch resistance is important.

Farmhouse or Belfast sinks are among the most popular ranges in ceramic. More common in Europe, these large sinks can be expensive and are heavy to handle.

Vitreous enamel, polycarbonate and a range of sinks moulded from man-made composites are available to suit every requirement and fit every kitchen. Some sinks are single drainer and some are double drainer; there are single bowls and double bowls. Some have one and a half bowls and some include chopping boards and baskets, the range available is both colourful and extensive.

When eventually you have selected the sink that best suits your kitchen, you need to decide the 'hand' that suits you best – that is, which side the sink 'drainer' is situated. This will then affect the positions and therefore the purposes of the adjacent kitchen units. Plumbing for the taps and drainage facilities must also be attached including, where required, a waste disposal unit. Then finally before using the sink if it is stainless steel, brass or enamel, it must be 'earthed' by a qualified electrician to reduce the risk of an electric shock.

As well as kitchen sinks, kitchen taps are available in a huge range of colours, shapes and sizes. They are available in brass, chromium and painted finishes. They may be single pillar taps supplying hot or cold water in a singular position or mixer taps where hot and cold water combine prior to discharge through a swivel head. In addition there are new taps for the elderly and the disabled, taps with screw tops and taps with lever tops and many other varieties. What is important is that your taps should be effective in their distribution of water and attractive in style, because they will form part of the focal point of your kitchen.

A Belfast sink adds a European touch.

Using that awkward corner in a practical way.

29

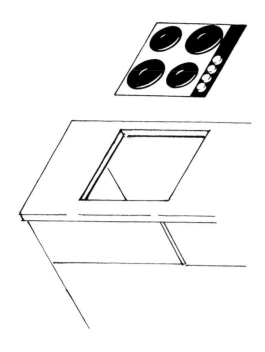

A hob unit can be inserted into a 'hole' cut into a worktop.

ACCESSORIES AND APPLIANCES

The selection of kitchen accessories and appliances will be central to the design and layout of your new kitchen and it will also determine what the kitchen will be used for and what services are to be included. Where all kitchen functions including cooking and laundering are to be carried out within the same area then the location of appliances such as a washing machine and a tumble drier will be vital. If the kitchen does not have the luxury of a utility room where this laundering activity can be carried out then the demands upon the kitchen space will be greater. And of course where room is required for both the preparation and eating of meals then demands on the space will be even greater. Carrying out all these activities within one area not only requires a great deal of careful planning and design in the initial stages but also later on in the execution of them for the kitchen to work effectively.

Kitchen appliances are available as 'free-standing' and 'built in' units. Free-standing appliances such as a cooker and a fridge/freezer can be catered for by simply leaving a gap, between the floor units and wall units, where that particular appliance is to stand. But it is not just a case of leaving gaps for these appliances to be slotted

(Right) Manufacturers ensure that kitchen appliances such as fridges fit snugly into units.

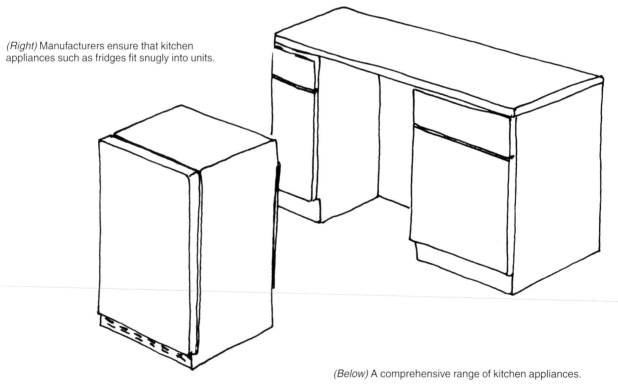

(Below) A comprehensive range of kitchen appliances.

(Above) A built-in electric hob unit.

(Right) Single ovens are designed to fit under work surfaces.

Tall units are made to receive appliances such as cookers and are designed to ventilate the appliance.

Appliances can be fitted with doors to suit the kitchen unit style.

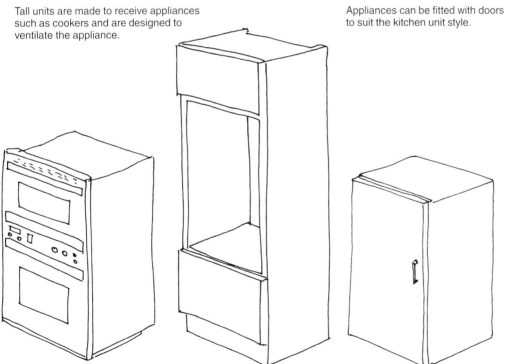

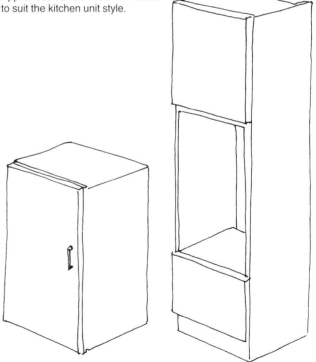

into, adjacent floor and wall units and services such as electricity must be planned to accommodate them. This also applies to built-in appliances. They are becoming more common and, in some cases, the appliances can be disguised to look like any other kitchen cabinet. Of course you may not want to camouflage an appliance, you may want it to stand out or, from the various colours available, to highlight and complement your new kitchen. Whatever your reason or selection, manufacturers have been quick to realize how important it is to build appliances of a uniform height, width and depth so that they can easily be included when kitchens are being planned.

Of course, the most important appliance in any kitchen is the cooker. Available as a free-standing unit or with a built-in oven and hob the kitchen cooker can be as simple or elaborate as your pocket can afford. Fuel selection may well reduce possibilities depending upon the type of fuel available. The majority of modern kitchens favour gas and electricity though both solid fuel and 'calor' gas bear

(Above) Install a cooker hood to banish all the cooking odours and condensation from the kitchen.

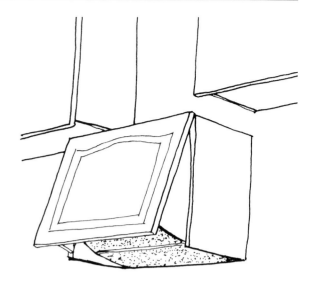

A cooker hood fitted between a run of wall units.

(Below) Fitting a Wickes cooker hood ventilation.

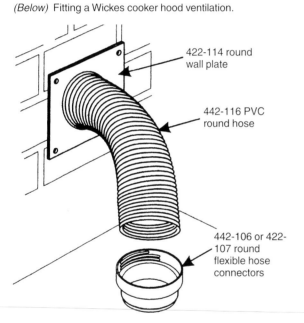

422-114 round wall plate

442-116 PVC round hose

442-106 or 422-107 round flexible hose connectors

consideration in areas where choice is limited. Some cookers even use two separate fuels – for example, it is quite possible to have a gas hob and an electric oven. When you have decided your fuel preferences then you will need to decide whether you prefer a free-standing cooker or a built-in oven and hob unit. Built-in appliances will allow you to site the oven and the hob in completely different locations within the kitchen, but always apply the rules of the work triangle when positioning these.

Of course, the traditional country-kitchen look will be enhanced by the inclusion of a traditional cooker and there is no more traditional cooker than the cast iron 'range'. Now becoming increasingly popular and fashionable, these large appliances run on all modern fuels and can also be used to assist the central heating system. An early decision about including a range in your kitchen is important because the kitchen will need to be designed around these heavyweight units.

Cooker hoods to recirculate cleaned air back into the kitchen or to extract it through an outside vent fulfil a vital role in the kitchen. Integrated hoods, where the air is cleaned before recirculating, will contain paper, metal or charcoal filters where grease and cooking

Cooker Hood Top

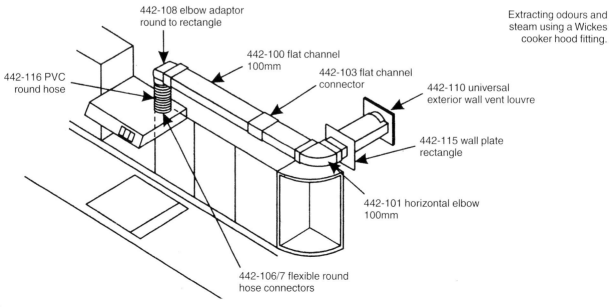

442-108 elbow adaptor round to rectangle

442-100 flat channel 100mm

442-103 flat channel connector

442-116 PVC round hose

442-110 universal exterior wall vent louvre

442-115 wall plate rectangle

442-101 horizontal elbow 100mm

442-106/7 flexible round hose connectors

Extracting odours and steam using a Wickes cooker hood fitting.

Making wood work: a superb kitchen wallrack.

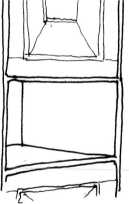

(Above left) Built-in double ovens are both versatile and convenient to use.

(Above) The fridge can store food effectively and be in keeping with any kitchen style.

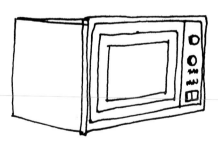

Microwaves play an important role in the kitchen of today.

odours can be suitably extracted. The filters must be checked and cleaned at regular intervals to maintain a clean environment. Chimney extractors will also contain grease filters, but the air will be dispersed through an outside vent and not recirculated into the kitchen.

Second only to the cooker will be a fridge and freezer unit. These can be installed under the worktop or fitted into a tall unit. The fronts can be camouflaged to suit the kitchen décor and, because operational switches are not surface mounted as they are with dishwashers, the fridge and freezer can be completely concealed. If your plan is to have a visible unit then the range of colours is very extensive. Large fridge and fridge/freezer units can be installed as tall units or can be stacked one on top of the other. The only real consideration when positioning a fridge or freezer is where it fits into the work triangle, and the only service required will be an electrical power point or fused spur.

The latest but not the least important kitchen appliance is the microwave oven. Advances in technology and reduction in prices due to competition has projected this into almost every modern kitchen where it will play a vital role. This appliance is also being catered for in kitchen unit design with tall units available for housing a microwave oven. Small and compact, the majority of kitchens will include a free standing unit sitting neatly on a worktop in the most advantageous position for usage.

Another appliance that is extremely popular in the modern kitchen and is no longer considered a luxury is the dishwasher. There is no longer any need to wash dishes by hand and, from a practical point of view, dishwashers have proven to be cleaner, more hygienic and more economical than hand washing. One of the reasons for improved hygiene is that the water temperature is greater in a dishwasher and a second reason is that the risk of spreading germs from a hand towel is eliminated.

The efficient storage of ingredients and household items help in the organization of everyday life.

The running of your kitchen can be so much more efficient.

Dishwashers have been designed to fit into any single unit space and door fronts can be designed to match the kitchen units. Installation of this appliance should be fairly straightforward as long as it is positioned close to water feeds and adjacent to drainage outlets.

Washing machines may not be considered to be kitchen appliances, but for those houses lacking a separate utility room then the kitchen may be the only place for it. Front loading and top loading machines will require their own considerations as will stacking units. Saving space by putting a tumble drier on top of a washing machine is also fairly common. When space is at an absolute premium perhaps a combined washer/tumble drier should be considered. But, whatever your decision, as with the dishwasher, water feeds and drainage outlets will dictate positioning. Some washing machines, particularly those built outside the UK, are cold feed only and some are both hot and cold feed.

Smaller electrical gadgets including electric whiskers and blenders, coffee machines and toasters are but a few of the multitude to be considered when planning worktop space and electrical point positions. Other accessories also important for the smooth running of your kitchen that need to be considered when you make your plans are waste bins, towel rails, a vegetable rack, a saucepan rack, a spice rack and a wine rack.

WASTE DISPOSAL

An increasingly essential part of any kitchen and the next step from effective dishwashing is the inclusion of a waste disposal unit. With approximately 25 per cent of household waste being food items increasing the risk of smells and the attraction of insects and bacteria, quick and effective disposal is extremely desirable. A waste disposal unit is easy to install requiring both plumbing and electrical installation. Of course where electricity and water are concerned the greatest care must be taken and the siting of switches given extra consideration.

FLOORING

The choice of flooring available today is quite staggering. Flagstones, wooden strips, ceramic tiles, marble, vinyl sheets and carpets figure highly in the range of possibilities, but the key to selection is in the suitability of your choice for the area in which it is to be used. The materials used for a kitchen floor should be easy to clean, durable and attractive to look at. A great deal of time is spent in and around the kitchen so appearance, possibly over a long period of time, is a prime consideration. Another consideration is that, with the kitchen being the second wettest room in the house, next to the bathroom, the floor must be water resistant and where porous materials such as wood are used they must be sealed according to manufacturer's instructions. Much more suitable are hard-wearing materials such as stone, quarry tiles and ceramic tiles that, when sealed properly, will fulfil nearly all the criteria required and provide an attractive end product. Water-absorbent materials such as carpets are not best used in this environment and could be dangerous.

Stone is a natural flooring material, it is extremely hard wearing and, although expensive, requires little aftercare and should last a lifetime. A stone floor should be sealed, after it is laid, with a suitable water-based sealant but be sure to check what effect the sealant has on the natural floor colour before using it.

Quarry tiles, traditional flooring in kitchens, are ideal. They are made from high silica alumina clay then fired for hardness. A quarry tile floor can be laid directly onto

Well-planned floor and wall features can create a superb traditional effect.

the existing floor screed but be sure to check what effect the additional thickness will have on the operation of doors and other fixtures. When laid the quarry tiles will be grouted using a cement-based grout. Do not leave excess grout on the tiles to dry out as it may leave an unwanted stain. Quarry tiles are easy to clean and water-resistant when sealed properly.

An alternative floor covering to stone and quarry tiles is ceramic floor tiles. Slimmer than either stone or quarry tiles these increasingly popular floor coverings are available in a wide range of sizes, colours and patterns. They are hard-wearing and have a glazed finish. And, of course, with so much walking about done in the work area of the kitchen a non-slip surface is vital. One drawback with using ceramic tiles is that wear-and-tear and damage does not improve the floor and, being less dense than the other hard floor coverings, the surface of the tiles can easily be chipped or cracked. When a tile is cracked it should be removed and a replacement fitted in order to retain the overall effect.

Vinyl flooring is a very popular and easy to lay floor covering. It is available in both sheet and tile form, in a wide variety of colours and patterns and also with a cushioned effect. When compared with stone and ceramic tiles a vinyl floor will be a lot cheaper to install; it will also be easier on the feet than the harder alternatives but it will not have the same lasting effect. If you do choose vinyl flooring and you are not sure whether to use tiles or sheet vinyl then you must first consider what wear the floor is likely to endure. If the kitchen is used regularly and some areas will be used more than others then tiles may be the best bet. Vinyl does wear with traffic and where sheet vinyl is used the whole floor would need to be replaced, unlike tiles where only the worn tiles would need replacing. With this point in mind be sure to buy a few 'extra' tiles just in case the colour and style you choose becomes a discontinued line.

Stone, quarry tiles and ceramic tiles and vinyl are all ideal kitchen floor coverings and are easy to clean and maintain. Installation though is rather a different matter. A new stone floor will require a great deal of preparation including selection of materials and possible excavation works. This is definitely a job for the professionals. Tiles, both quarry and ceramic, can be laid by the competent do-it-yourself enthusiast but a great deal of planning is required to achieve the best results. Vinyl flooring and vinyl tiles are much simpler floor coverings and are both easy to cut, a sharp knife or a pair of scissors should suffice, and easy to lay. Errors can be replaced when laying tiles but are not so easy when laying the sheet vinyl flooring.

Kitchen floors, like bathroom floors, are not the best environments for water-absorbent materials such as carpets where they will be difficult to keep hygienically clean and dry and could be dangerous. Carpet tiles, on the other hand, are available for this particular purpose and for use in this special environment. It is important though, when using carpet tiles, that they are secured to the surface using a proprietary double-sided tape or

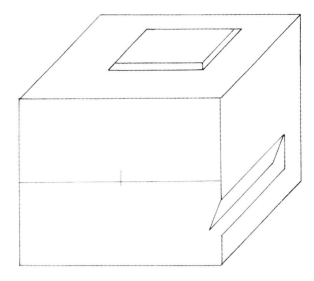

Find the centre line of the floor.

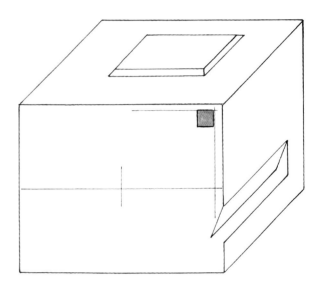

Begin near the corner following the guide marks made.

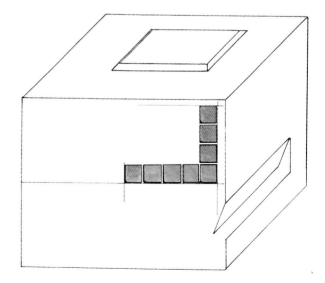

Space out the tiles to find the corner of the room.

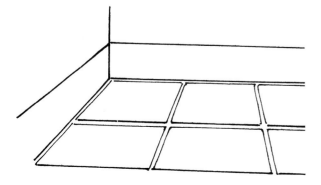

(Left) Typical floor tile layout.

The central focus of any kitchen, a solid kitchen table.

glue to ensure stability and safety. And of course when the tiles are stained or soiled they can be easily replaced. Like vinyl tiles and sheet vinyl floor coverings carpet tiles are easy to install by the competent amateur.

WALL TILES

The use of wall tiles in the kitchen area will normally be restricted to a splash back behind the sink and any adjacent work surfaces. Where and to what extent the wall tiles will be used, the principles will remain the same. Wall tiles are a hard-wearing, decorative and easy-to-clean surface absolutely ideal for kitchen areas. There is an enormous selection to choose from that will include shape, style and colour. There are plain and decorative styles and there are regular and irregular shapes. Whatever the choice the tiles should be selected to be compatible with the style of kitchen and not clash with the planned floor covering.

And of course the installation of wall tiles has never been easier. Special cutting tools can be bought along with fixing materials, while fitting instructions are readily available and easy to follow.

For inexperienced wall tilers the most important points to follow are:

1. to plan carefully making sure the lines are horizontal and vertical using a spirit level;
2. to immediately remove excess adhesive from the face of tiles when they are pressed into place;
3. to immediately remove excess grout from the face of the tiles when grouting in.

(Below) Wall tiling.

Kitchen Planner Data Sheet (Page 76)

Step by Step
1) Transfer the measurements of your Kitchen area to the grid sheet.
2) For each measurement take more than one reading.
3) Allow for any discrepancies when adding the measurements to the grid.
4) Add the positions of all services (for example, Gas, Electricity and Water).

The Work Triangle
1) Do not interrupt the work triangle with tall units.
2) Always position floor units below wall units.
3) Make sure regularly used storage areas are accessible.

Electrics
1) Each major electrical appliance must have its own fused outlet.
2) Allow at least *six* extra power points for kitchen appliances, kettles and so on.
3) Do not position power points too close to sinks.
4) Adequate lighting is important.
5) Do not position the cooker close to doors.

BATHROOM PLANNING

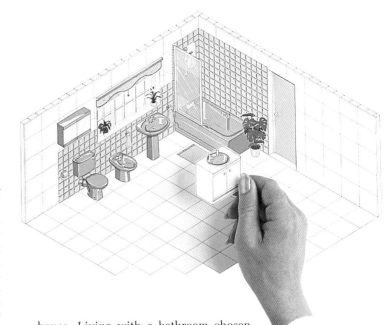

Although it was back in the 1920s and 1930s that the changing attitudes towards health and hygiene first led to the bathroom being considered an essential part of every home, it is only in the last two decades that it has become such a focus of attention. The toilet has come a long way since it was a 'privy' at the bottom of the garden and the bath is no longer a 'tub' you sit in, in front of the fire. Nor is the bathroom now just thought of as an essential room where you find a bath, a washbasin and a toilet – it has become much more functional. It is a room that, thanks to a revolution in style and design, can be efficient, attractive, comfortable and hygienic. Add to this the fact that developments in the materials used in manufacture have led to a far greater flexibility in the colour and style of your bathroom suite and you will see how dramatic the changes have been in recent years.

Today's bathroom is all about comfort, colour and practicality. It is a place where you can freshen up at the start of the day or relax at the end of it. The style can be modern or Victorian, the colour can be pastel or vivid and the room can be small or large making the possibilities almost endless. No longer is the bathroom a dreary, steamy room to be used only as a basic amenity, a room for a quick wash and brush up.

Changing your bathroom will usually be for one of four possible reasons. The first is when you move into a new house. Living with a bathroom chosen and used by someone else is not always an acceptable option. The majority of home movers will want to style the kitchen and the bathroom to fit in with their own personal choices. The second reason for change is because the existing bathroom suite or tiling is cracked and stained or just showing its age and, with friends visiting our homes and using the bathroom, it has very much become a reflection of us. Having a second bathroom or a plush and stylish one is second in importance only to hygiene. The third reason is as part of a new, home extension. An increasing number of people extend their homes every year in order to create more living space for themselves and their families which allows them to expand without the upheaval of moving. This may mean adding to the existing bathroom, or possibly even creating a second bathroom. And the fourth reason is to keep up with the many changes in

A luxurious and understated bathroom suite.

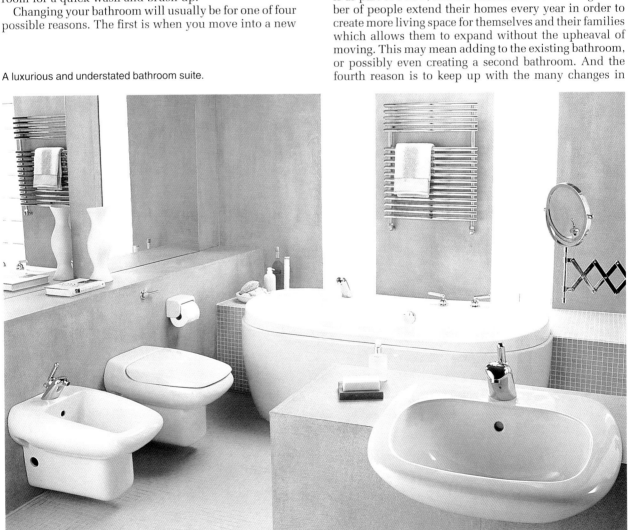

Bathroom Planning

The elegance of the Victorian era revived.

(Below) A bathroom suite with understated lines.

style and colour schemes that are reflected not only in our everyday life but also in the modern home.

Estate agents will tell you that they consider bathrooms to be second in importance only to kitchens when selling and buying a home and, fortunately, the cost of changing the bathroom need not be excessive.

If you are designing a bathroom from scratch, in a new extension for example, then you will find that the design possibilities are almost infinite. You should start by first approaching manufacturers for ideas and leaflets showing how their ranges can be used and what layout may prove to be most beneficial. You can visit showrooms where vast numbers of bathroom suites can be seen on display or you can call in a professional designer. Whatever you choose to do there are just a few points you will need to have clear in your mind that will assist the effectiveness of your layout. The first point is: who is to use the bathroom? You may want it to be purely functional or you may want it to be warm and seductive. The second point

(Above) Classical Florentine styling.

(Above) Beech-effect bathroom furniture.

(Right) The 'back-to-the-wall' style bathroom suite.

will be the age of the users: young children and the elderly may require special facilities to ensure that the bathroom can be used safely, efficiently and hygienically. And finally but also importantly you will need to know how much to spend on the bathroom. If you are adding or changing a bathroom prior to a house sale then you must ensure that the money is spent wisely and is not wasted.

LAYOUT

Before considering what layout is best for your new bathroom you must be clear in your mind why the existing layout is to be changed. What is wrong with the existing bathroom? Is it too small? Is it badly lit? Or is there little or no storage space for disinfectants and toilet rolls?

Maybe you want the bathroom to work more efficiently by changing the suite around – for example, by moving the loo to a better position, provided the drainage allows for this. Maybe the bath is in the wrong place and maybe the mirrors and towel rails are also in completely

Bathroom Planning

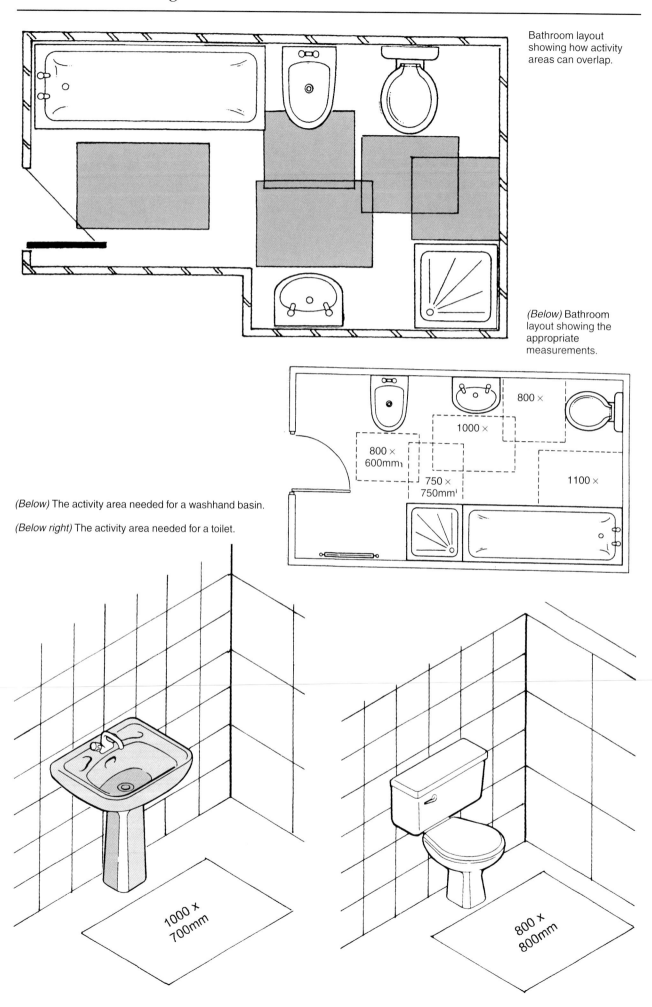

Bathroom layout showing how activity areas can overlap.

(Below) Bathroom layout showing the appropriate measurements.

800 ×

1000 ×

800 ×
600mm

750 ×
750mm

1100 ×

(Below) The activity area needed for a washhand basin.

(Below right) The activity area needed for a toilet.

1000 ×
700mm

800 ×
800mm

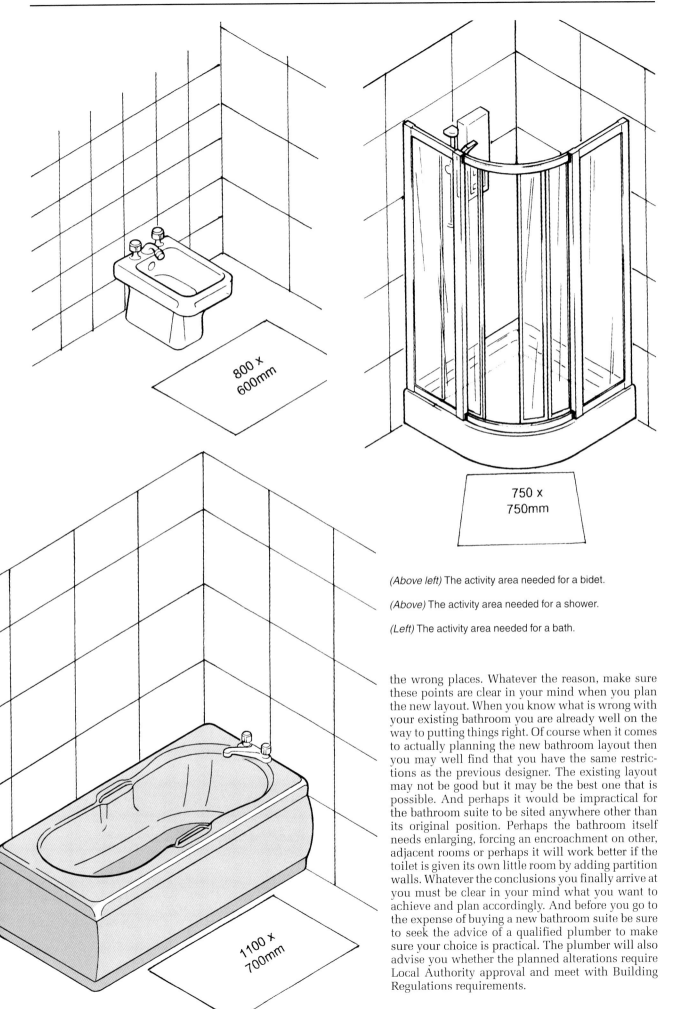

(Above left) The activity area needed for a bidet.

(Above) The activity area needed for a shower.

(Left) The activity area needed for a bath.

800 x 600mm

750 x 750mm

1100 x 700mm

the wrong places. Whatever the reason, make sure these points are clear in your mind when you plan the new layout. When you know what is wrong with your existing bathroom you are already well on the way to putting things right. Of course when it comes to actually planning the new bathroom layout then you may well find that you have the same restrictions as the previous designer. The existing layout may not be good but it may be the best one that is possible. And perhaps it would be impractical for the bathroom suite to be sited anywhere other than its original position. Perhaps the bathroom itself needs enlarging, forcing an encroachment on other, adjacent rooms or perhaps it will work better if the toilet is given its own little room by adding partition walls. Whatever the conclusions you finally arrive at you must be clear in your mind what you want to achieve and plan accordingly. And before you go to the expense of buying a new bathroom suite be sure to seek the advice of a qualified plumber to make sure your choice is practical. The plumber will also advise you whether the planned alterations require Local Authority approval and meet with Building Regulations requirements.

Before deciding where to put the new suite measure the area carefully.

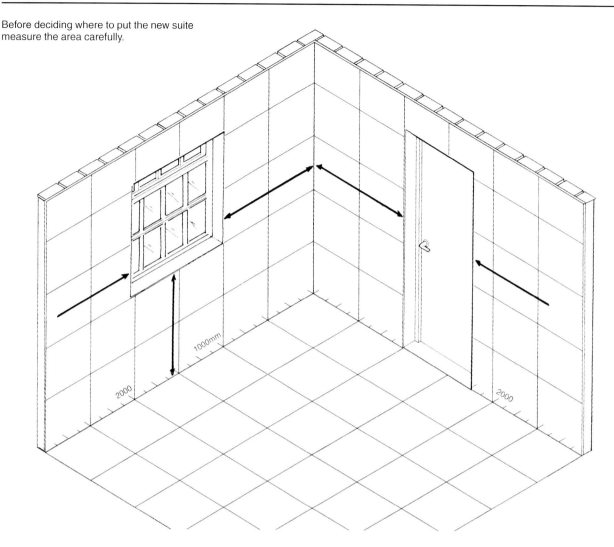

MEASURING UP

When you plan the new bathroom it is no good trying to use every inch of space or trying to cram everything in. It will be just bad planning if you find yourself squeezing past the washbasin to get to the toilet or you are unable to reach the towel rail from the bath. Careful measuring will ensure that the 'ergonomics' of the bathroom work properly and effectively. As with the kitchen, each unit will require its own 'user' space even if that 'user' space encroaches on other 'user' spaces within the bathroom.

To make a plan you will require a suitably sized sheet of graph paper, a pencil and a measure. Measure in metric, and always measure twice for accuracy and take more than one reading because not all rooms are square, then add the room dimensions to the graph paper including the position of doors and windows. From the existing bathroom suite positions you will then be able to add where the drainage pipes are positioned and where the hot and cold water services are. These positions, drainage and water pipe, can be altered but advice from a qualified professional is best sought before final decisions are made.

Working to the scale you have selected you can then make cut-outs of the appliances you want installed and their 'user' areas. Bearing in mind the services, you can then move these appliances around until you find a layout that is both sensible and workable. If you find, from moving things around, that there is just not enough room to accommodate your requirements then it may be time to look for space elsewhere. If the bathroom has an airing cupboard maybe it can be relocated on to the landing. Perhaps the shower can be accessed through a bedroom and maybe the toilet can have its

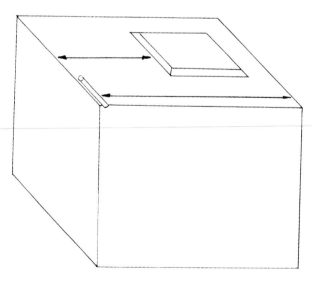

The location of plumbing fittings and drainage outlets will be crucial.

own cubicle adjacent to the bathroom. All these points must be considered if you want to maximize the space available. Seek the advice of a plumber about adding extra facilities. The plumber will tell you if there is enough water pressure for a shower and whether the existing system can cope. A good plumber will prove invaluable in this instance even if the advice adds a little to the overall cost. The fact that all the facilities

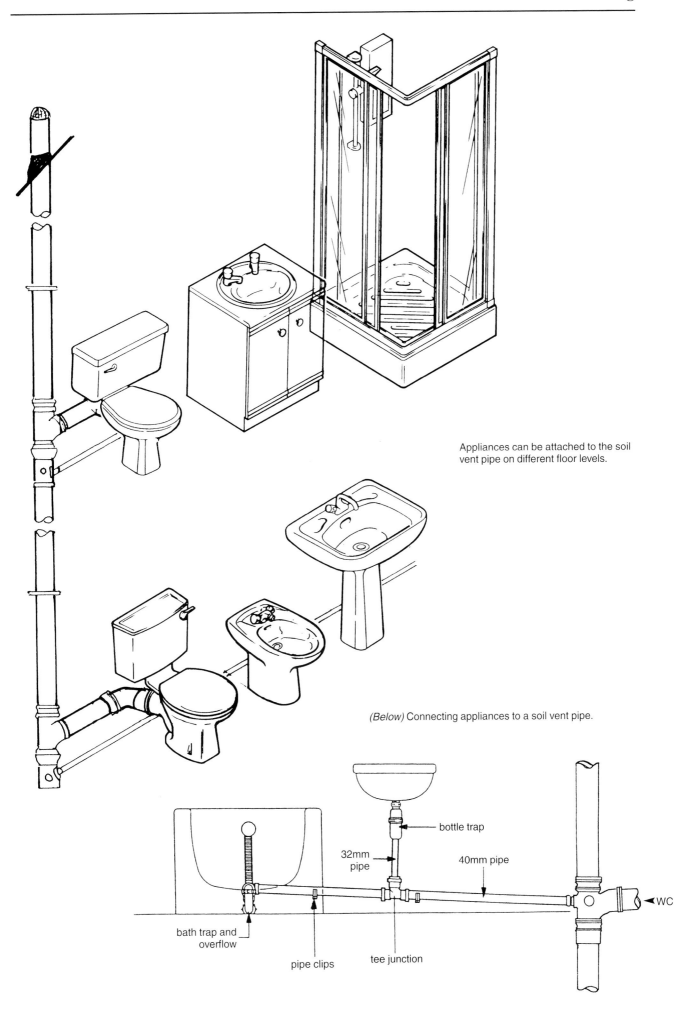

Appliances can be attached to the soil vent pipe on different floor levels.

(Below) Connecting appliances to a soil vent pipe.

bottle trap

32mm pipe

40mm pipe

WC

bath trap and overflow

pipe clips

tee junction

A toilet with a 'p' trap.

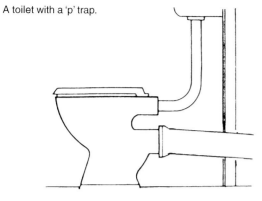

A toilet with an 's' trap.

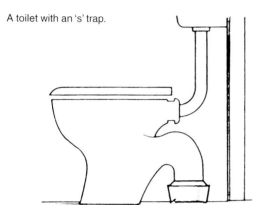

function to the best of their abilities will be reward enough.

Of course if the existing bathroom is large and floor space is not at a premium the layout will be easier to plan, but it will also need to be practical.

MAKING A CHOICE

There is an extensive range of bathroom equipment to choose from to meet almost every style and suit almost every budget. Suites are available in all materials including acrylic, glass fibre, steel and cast iron. The appliances can be streamlined and modern or period and traditional. Baths can be standard or corner and with or without whirlpool facilities. Washhand basins come with and without a pedestal and toilets may be close coupled and with or without a syphonic flush action. Adding a shower will mean fitting a curtain or shower screen to the bath or installing an independent unit with a shower tray and a surround. Taps are available in a variety of styles and finishes designed to complement the appliances and add a touch of glamour where required.

There is an art to selecting the right suite and the right accessories but help will always be on hand from interested manufacturers and the DIY superstores. After you have chosen the appliances that best meet your requirements, the material of the new bathroom suite and the

Position appliances on a grid sheet for accuracy.

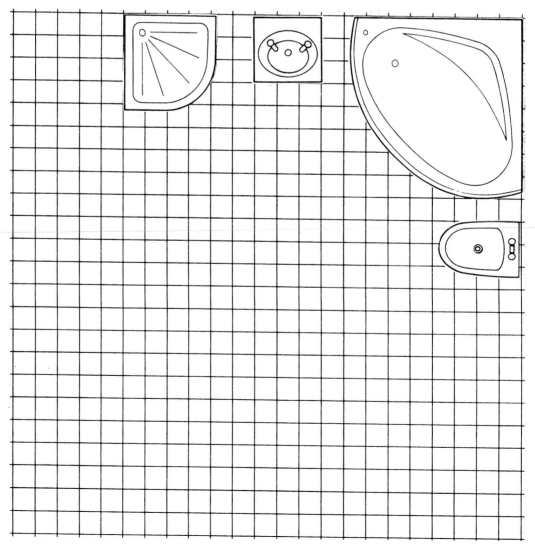

(Right) The craftsmanship of the past and the luxury of the present.

style, contemporary or traditional, there is the colour to consider. And the range of available colours may be vast. You may well have selected a colour scheme for your new bathroom before you selected a suite, but ultimately the colour scheme will be determined by the colour of suite you choose.

Long gone are the days when white was virtually the only 'colour' available, bathroom suites are now available in almost any colour you care to mention. Light colours can make a room seem larger than it really is and bright colours can warm a room up. Blue is traditional with bathrooms but it can 'cool' a room quite dramatically.

THE BATH

The bathroom suite will undoubtedly be the most expensive purchase you will have to make so seek any worthwhile advice you can before doing so. The bath, for instance, will be available in a wide range of sizes. You may want to opt for extra length and extra width, where the room is available, but make sure your water system can cope with any extra demand. The bath could be cast iron, pressed steel, acrylic or fibreglass. Cast iron and pressed steel baths are long-lasting, they hold the water temperature well and do not creak when in use. A pressed steel bath has all the advantages of a cast

Bathroom opulence.

Simply stunning with pure, clean, simple lines.

A classic for connoisseurs.

(Below left) An ocean of ideas.

(Below) An inset oval bath. No compromise on inspiration.

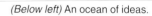

(Above) A 'slipper' bath.

(Right) A single-tap semi-pedestal basin.

(Below) Use every inch of space with this 'back-to-the-wall' bathroom suite.

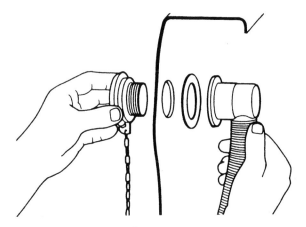

Assembling a flexible overflow.

iron bath and will also be less expensive. On the negative side metal baths are heavy, expensive and take time to warm up.

Acrylic and fibreglass baths are light and inexpensive. They are warm to get into and available in a wide range of colours. On the negative side the cheaper versions can distort and move away from the wall when in use and the surface may be easily scratched.

The shape of baths has also changed dramatically over recent years with long baths, short baths, corner baths and round baths to choose from. Bath panels to match the style and colour of the bath will be available for the sides and the ends. On the other hand, if the bath is to be boxed in, then the surround may be made from carpet or ceramic tiles to suit the location and the mood.

Whirlpool baths and jacuzzis used to be available only to the very rich but these spa baths are now available in a wide range to suit almost any pocket and fit almost any shaped bath.

The new bath is likely to have handgrips on either side to assist entry and exit from the bath to help the young and not-so-young user. It may also have a non-slip bottom, essential if you are considering adding a shower attachment.

THE BASIN

The choice of basin, as part of a suite, will normally be limited to size and style. The size you choose should be determined by what the basin is to be used for. If it is to be multifunctional coping with hair-washing and shaving then a larger size may be the best option. If, on the other hand, it is to be used purely for hand washing then perhaps a smaller size will be appropriate. The style you choose will rest between a pedestal basin, a wall hung basin or a vanity style basin. The pedestal basin will be ideal for concealing waste and water pipes. The wall hung basin will leave more floor space but the water pipes and drainage pipe will be visible and the vanity basin will have the basin sunk into a flat work surface with a boxed surround forming a vanity unit. A vanity unit will also be ideal for bedrooms where towels and so forth can be stored out of sight.

WC

The lavatory basin will invariably be made from vitreous china in a variety of shapes and sizes with high level, low level or close-coupled cisterns. A close-coupled cistern is where the cistern is attached to the basin forming a single unit. All the cisterns will be wall-mounted with some concealed behind a false wall or panelling. The action of the cistern to flush down the basin can be a standard washdown action or a syphonic action. The syphonic action is quieter and may be recommended where en-suite facilities are being added or where the bathroom is situated close to guest rooms. The syphonic system is only available with close-coupled units.

BIDET

The bidet is becoming more and more a part of the British bathroom. Popular on the Continent, the bidet is important for personal hygiene and, like the toilet, can be free standing or fixed back against a wall. The taps can be fitted with or without a spray facility so check with you local water authority for the type they recommend. In some areas they may not accept the type with the ascending spray.

SHOWER

Adding a new shower will add greatly to the bathroom's functions. It is very handy having a shower as well as a bath, and a shower uses only a quarter of the water it takes to fill a bath. The simplest option will be an over-the-bath shower but, if there is room, a separate shower will add an extra facility to your home.

To install an over-the-bath shower you will need to decide where the water is to come from. It can be supplied via mixer taps attached to the bath and served directly from the hot water system or, alternatively, you can fit a thermostatically controlled electric instantaneous

The curved shape and twin sliding doors make this shower enclosure ideal where space is at a premium.

(Above) A frameless pivot door enclosure.

(Right) A 'multi-spray' fitting for that all-over body shower.

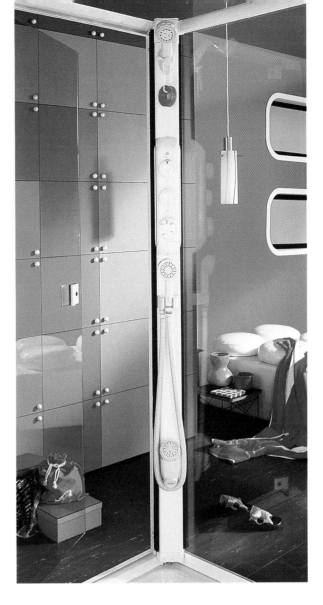

shower. This type of shower is fed by mains' cold water and heated by electricity. Being fed by the mains will mean that there should be sufficient water pressure for the shower to function properly and, being thermostatically controlled, there is less risk of scalding.

Mixer tap showers are less accurate. For the shower to operate properly there must be enough 'head' of water in the water tank to provide water pressure and there is always the risk of scalding when other facilities are used, such as running the cold tap or flushing the loo. To improve power to the shower where water pressure is weak a pump can be added to the system. The pump will operate instantaneously boosting the pressure of both the hot and the cold water supply to the shower mixers.

Over-the-bath showers need to be enclosed and can be screened using hanging plastic curtains or decorative plastic or glass screens. When selecting glass make sure that it is suitable for this purpose, and that it is safe and meets the appropriate British Standard requirements. Curtains are very popular for over-the-bath showers as they can easily be pulled aside when the shower is not in use.

Shower cubicles have come a long way over recent years and the choice available is very extensive. The shower tray can be cast iron, steel, acrylic or fibreglass and the screen surround may be glass, plastic or styrene. The shower tray must be adjusted to provide a secure and even balance when the shower is in use and the surround must be sealed along joints where it abuts walls or the shower base. Sealing a shower tray and cubicle properly will prevent problems at a later date.

Power showers and 'Jacuzzi' showers are becoming more and more popular. Assisted by a pump these showers can be more invigorating than a bath and occupy the same floor area as a standard shower cubicle. Water jets can be propelled at you from almost every conceivable direction and at a strength determined by the user.

JACUZZI WHIRLPOOL BATHS

The name 'Jacuzzi' is synonymous with whirlpool baths and has been a registered trademark for three decades. The 'Jacuzzi' whirlpool bath water jets provide a hydro massage 'treatment' for soothing the body and relaxing the mind. This effective hydrotherapy, recognized long ago by the healers in ancient India, claims to relieve the symptoms of back pain, arthritis, rheumatism and conditions

The deeply penetrating massaging power of the Jacuzzi jet.

This whirlpool bath will fit into the smallest bathroom.

A spacious corner whirlpool bath with supportive headrest.

A multifunctional showering and hydromassage centre.

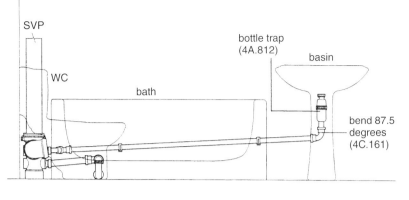

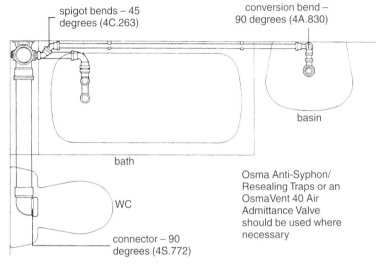

(Top) Basin taps.

(Above) A basin mixer tap.

A typical bathroom layout showing 'Osma' drainage fittings in use.

linked to blood flow, such as varicose veins. The 'jacuzzi' jets massaging the lumber region, legs and hips cause the blood vessels in the skin and underlying tissues to dilate. This allows the blood flow to increase and the cells to take in more oxygen yet, at the same time, allowing the pores to open and the skin to be cleansed of impurities. The result is improved circulation, the skin is toned and there is an overall glow of vitality. To install a 'jacuzzi' whirlpool bath or a 'jacuzzi' shower enclosure you will require a hot and cold water supply and a fused 13amp spur. If the water pressure is too low you may also require a booster pump of a size according to the manufacturer's specifications.

TAPS

Selecting taps to suit the new suite may be fairly straightforward but you must also take into consideration the users. Young children and the elderly may require special fittings to help them use these facilities properly. Mixer taps, where the hot and cold water is mixed together, can be fitted where a single lever controls the flow and the temperature. Mixer taps are also available in a style to suit the traditional-look bathroom where such taps would have been unlikely.

Taps and mixer taps are available in many shapes, colours and finishes: gold taps, chrome taps and brass taps; taps with onyx tops and plastic taps; washbasin and bath taps can include plungers for opening and closing the plug hole and bidet taps can include a spray. Selecting the design of tap that suits your circumstances

and the style of bathroom you are planning should be made at the same time as you select your suite. The fittings must be compatible and the style should match.

PLUMBING

Before making any decisions about suites or additional fittings check with a qualified plumber that your plans are both legal and feasible. Alterations to the cold and hot water systems may be required along with additions to the drains. Your existing water tanks may not be suitable for the purposes you are planning and the hot water boiler may need upgrading. Installing huge baths in peculiar locations may look good in catalogues and brochures but may be completely impractical in reality. The proximity of other rooms to the bathroom may dictate the location of a toilet and the position of the soil vent pipe may be crucial. For the inexperienced, trying to make major alterations to the layout of a bathroom without expert help or guidance could be a step too far. Plumbing fitting manufacturers, though, have wasted little time in recognizing how the DIY enthusiast is tackling more and more of the plumbing jobs around the home. Easy to install pipes and fittings are being introduced at regular intervals to make the task more DIY friendly although larger projects should always be discussed with a qualified professional.

Replacing a bathroom suite is one of the projects now regularly tackled by do-it-yourself enthusiasts with increasingly successful results. Removing and replacing a bath or a washhand basin will cause only minor

Bathroom Planning

(Right) An electric shower must be installed correctly.

(Below) Fitting timber studwork around the bath.

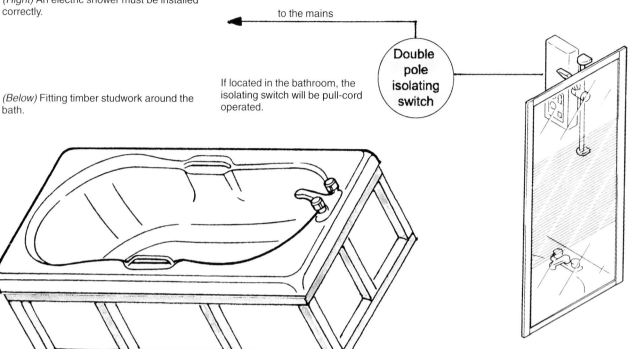

to the mains

Double pole isolating switch

If located in the bathroom, the isolating switch will be pull-cord operated.

A selection of Yorkshire solder ring fittings.

A selection of Tectite 'push-fit' plumbing and heating fittings.

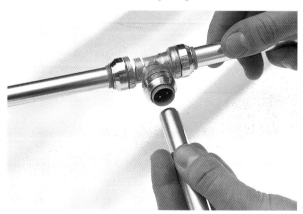

Tectite joints are assembled by hand without the need for tools, adhesives or pastes.

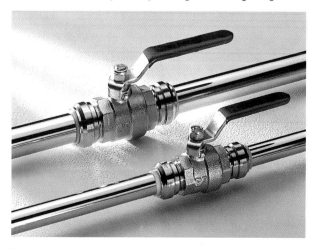

Tectite quarter-turn ball valves are ideal for hot and cold services and heating systems.

Bathroom lighting can be clean and fresh in the morning, calm and intimate in the evening.

Brighten up your shower with ceiling-mounted spotlights in waterproof-enclosed fittings.

inconvenience whereas replacing a toilet will need a little more careful planning. The new toilet trap will need to be the same as the existing toilet trap and, unless changes are to be made to the cold water supply, the cistern should be the same.

Adding new units to the existing facilities will also require careful planning. Installing a new cubicle shower or a bidet where none existed before will require connection to the hot and cold water supply and drainage pipes will need to be installed. Adding to the drainage outlets is no easy matter. It is important that the pipe runs are kept to a minimum and are well supported with brackets. Fitting a trap to a shower and then connecting the drainage pipe to the outlet pipes will also need to be planned carefully.

If the existing system is old then the pipes may be in imperial measurements. There are connectors and reducers to accommodate this but recognition before action will be important. Cutting off the water supply only to find out you do not have the correct fittings will not make for a happy household so, if you are at all unsure, seek the advice and help of a local plumber. Then if everything goes pear-shaped you may have an experienced professional to turn to for assistance.

Replacing a toilet should be a fairly simple task if you prepare for it correctly. Make sure you have the correct fittings and the correct sanitary ware before you turn off the cold water supply. The cistern can be flushed just the once to empty it. If the old cistern is an independent unit, not connected to the toilet bowl, the water supply pipe and overflow pipe can be disconnected and then it can be removed from the wall. Then a replacement cistern can be easily fitted by simply retracing your steps. Make sure the plumbing fittings are tight. To remove a toilet bowl after the cistern is disconnected you simply unscrew the floor fittings and lift it from the drain connector. Replacing a bowl is the reverse. If the drain connector does not match the new bowl a 'multikwik' drain connector may be required. Be sure to push the bowl connection tightly into the drain to form a firm joint. Removing and replacing a close-coupled unit is the same except that the cistern and the toilet bowl are connected.

ELECTRICS

Electricity in the bathroom will require careful planning and is not really a do-it-yourself installation. Among the fittings requiring electricity are showers, shaver points and lights. Instant electric showers will be connected through a fused spur with possibly a pull switch to activate it. It will invariably work off a cold water supply only. A shaver point, usually part of a light fitting, can be connected to the lighting ring main along with the light fittings or via the power point ring main off a fused spur and will be activated by a pull cord switch. Power points are not permitted in bathrooms for safety reasons and light switches will be ceiling mounted and pull cord operated. Power for wall heaters will be supplied, like the electric shower connection, from the ring main and through a fused spur. All the switches in the bathroom, including wall heater switches and extractor fans, should be pull cord switches. Light fittings will also need to be suitable for bathroom use. Special ceiling, mounted units, where the bulbs are enclosed, are very popular, as are recessed spotlights.

Fitting electric showers has become very popular and is a job for a professional electrician. The showers are relatively quick and easy to install requiring only a cold water feed for supply and then activated by a pull cord switch. The electricity supply will be similar to that used for the cooker with its own circuit and an isolating switch between the shower unit and the consumer unit. Before connecting the shower, make sure the cable and fittings are suitable to cope with the shower's wattage and then, when the shower is installed and ready for use, make sure the supply pipework is 'earthed'. Electric wall heaters and towel rails can be installed in bathrooms but they must be fitted correctly. Switches for these units should be placed outside the bathroom, or, when they are in the bathroom a cord-operated switch should be used. Again all metallic parts of these fittings must be included in the earth bonding of the bathroom unit.

Making a mistake with the plumbing in the bathroom can result in wet patches but making a mistake with the electricity can kill.

LIGHTING

Bathroom designers will tell you that lighting is the single most important factor in creating the effect you want. Some may even say you should plan the lighting

first and the layout second. You only have to look at catalogues to see how important lighting is. Good lighting can totally transform the bathroom, probably more so than any other room in the house, and, because installing the lighting generally means structural work to walls and ceilings, it will be a good idea to discuss your plans with an electrician before you start. Fortunately advances in technology and the availability of almost any fitting means that you can illuminate the whole or part of certain areas, around mirrors for example, without breaking the bank.

The imaginative use of light in the bathroom lighting will play a very important part in mood creation whether you desire a romantic, dramatic or comfortable effect. Bright lighting will be important for activities such as shaving whereas gentle lighting will be perfect for lazing in the bath. Ceiling-mounted lights are traditional but hidden and unobtrusive lights may be more acceptable. Lights around the mirror or under cabinets and spotlights will be ideal for directing light where you want it and wall lights, up-lighters and down-lighters will be perfect for creating moods in a steamy environment. And, of course, all the fittings must be safe for use in bathrooms and sealed against condensation and moisture. As important as the fittings are they will be of no use if the bulbs are not suitable. Tungsten filament lighting will help to achieve a near daylight effect and low-voltage halogen bulbs will be perfect in spotlights. The bulbs must be suitable for use in bathrooms so check with the supplier for suitability.

Natural light is also important though the bathroom window of today, with its obscure glass and limited size, has been overlooked where natural light is concerned. Try not to shut out light by using curtains or blinds, use see-through materials that will allow the natural light to flood in while protecting your mystique. Large windows will help enormously and so will the position of mirrors, dispersing any natural daylight around the room.

(Above) A traditional towel rail radiator.

(Below) A stylish and modern radiator/towel rail.

(Below right) Adding another dimension to the bathroom.

(Above) A taste of the country.

(Right) A compact WC and basin can create a fully functioning and attractive cloakroom.

ACCESSORIES AND APPLIANCES

Unlike the modern kitchen the bathroom is not likely to be inundated with accessories or appliances. A bathroom suite will consist of a toilet, a bath and a washhand basin and some will include a bidet. The only other significant appliance is a shower unit. These five appliances should be positioned around the bathroom according to the location of doors, windows and services.

Accessories, unlike those in the kitchen, do not require well-placed worktops for them to be used. The majority of accessories in the kitchen require electricity, such as a kettle and a toaster. In the bathroom, accessories include linen baskets and chairs, mirrors and toothbrush holders, rugs and toilet seat covers, shelves for cosmetics and a medicine cabinet. The position of these accessories is not particularly vital to the smooth running of the bathroom but they do add to its ability to function properly. Back to the wall bathroom fittings may help to create shelving and cupboards for the storage of towels and toilet rolls. Vanity basins will provide the same service. Planning your bathroom to accommodate a new suite is part of the solution. Creating visible and hidden storage areas will follow on when the suite is in place.

Large mirrors will not only reflect the light, they will also make the bathroom appear larger. But make sure the mirrors are positioned to reflect the light into the room and not into your face, and they are at the right height for doing make-up or shaving.

And finally an accessory not really classified as a bathroom essential but that is creeping into our houses in greater numbers – plants. The bathroom area works wonderfully for some plants and terribly for others, but they are often used in manufacturers' promotional literature and add an extra splash of colour to contrast with the existing fittings.

THE DOWNSTAIRS LOO

Many modern houses are now being built with the inclusion of a downstairs toilet. Unlike the 'privy' at the bottom of the garden and more likely to be used by our visitors, this 'little' room will be just big enough to include a toilet and a washhand basin. And the downstairs loo will be ideal for saving the legs of elderly relatives or for the use of young children when they are playing in the garden.

If you do not already have a downstairs loo or cloakroom, then perhaps there is room to install one. Before you think too seriously about it you should check with your local Planning Department for advice and, if you do go ahead, then the work may need to be inspected by the Building Inspector. When completed, I am sure you will wonder how on earth you ever managed without it.

Of course to add a toilet and washhand basin to the existing services the drains need to be close by along with the hot and cold water pipes. If you build it under the stairs, a common location, headroom must be available as well as ventilation. Where there is no room for a window an electrical extractor fan will be required and light fittings added. Perhaps smaller sanitary units would be suitable, creating an appearance of space where in fact it is limited, but do not try to make room where there is none. A cramped and unwelcoming room is not advisable.

When planning the downstairs loo try to allow room for a radiator and a clothes rail for hanging damp clothing. With the majority of falls and cuts and grazes happening outside or in the garden perhaps there is room for a medicine cabinet to keep the plasters and bandages, but be sure to keep it out of the reach of young children.

Add wall tiles, flooring, curtains and the odd picture or plant and a room has been created that will be both functional and extremely welcoming to visitors.

EN-SUITE FACILITIES

As families grow up the need for more and adequate bathroom facilities will also grow and the answer may be an en-suite bathroom. This facility can be added to the main or master bedroom providing there is sufficient floor space for it. En-suite facilities may simply be a toilet and a small washhand basin to provide easy access to washing facilities or they may be a completely luxurious escape from reality, that is, a room designed completely from scratch without the limitations of the existing bathroom. The width and depth will be whatever you want them to be providing you have the space. And of course available drainage must be high on the list of priorities.

Drainage for an en-suite bathroom will need to meet the same building requirements imposed on any other drainage facility in the house and, where additions to the existing drains are concerned, must get Building Regulations approval. Where it is not possible to connect the en-suite facility to the existing drainage system a new soil vent pipe can be added and, when exiting the building, can be joined into the existing drains. If you are at all unsure that this is possible ask your local building inspector for advice. Installing a new drainage system may be an additional cost but it will certainly allow more freedom when it comes to positioning the bathroom appliances. A completely free hand can permit excesses not allowed in the confines of your existing bathroom. A corner bath maybe, or even a sunken bath, a 'jacuzzi' shower and a bidet working in a blank area can be fun but the room must also work practically.

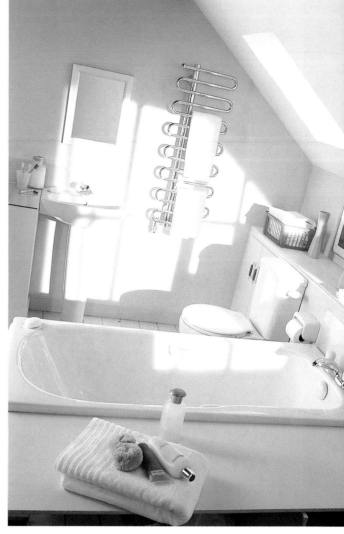

(Right) The height of convenience, a bathroom in the roofspace will add an extra dimension to any home.

(Below) Adding a bathroom to a bedroom has never been more popular.

(Right) Tiles and non-slip carpets add to the overall ambience of the bathroom.

NOISE REDUCTION

New houses are designed and bathroom appliances are positioned to reduce the noises emanating from bathrooms. The appliances will generally be secured to external walls and the partitions will be filled with sound-deadening materials. Where a new bathroom is adjacent to a bedroom, for example, or where a new en-suite room is built, sound-deadening material can be placed both under and above the partition to assist in noise reduction.

Newly built timber partitions should be filled with insulation quilt and then double tacked with plasterboard, the plasterboard joints being staggered. Additional care must be taken where the partition wall abuts other walls, the floor and the ceiling to ensure that the soundproof barrier is not compromised.

Newly installed soil vent pipes will be boxed in and an insulation material wrapped around the pipe to reduce noise. In fact any measure taken, whether in a new or an older dwelling, to reduce any noises from the bathroom will be beneficial to all members of the household and their visitors.

VENTILATION

To comply with Building Regulations the windows in a toilet must be of a size suitable to provide the ventilation required. In the event that the window ventilation

(Below) Clever planning may be essential when adding a touch of luxury in a limited space.

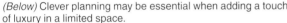

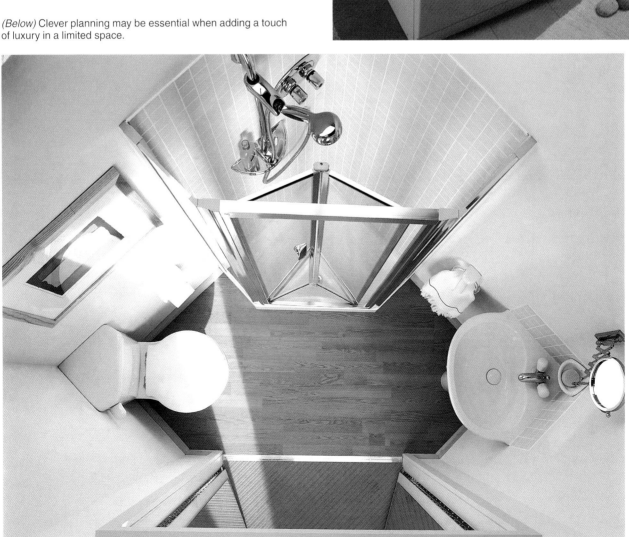

Bathroom Planning

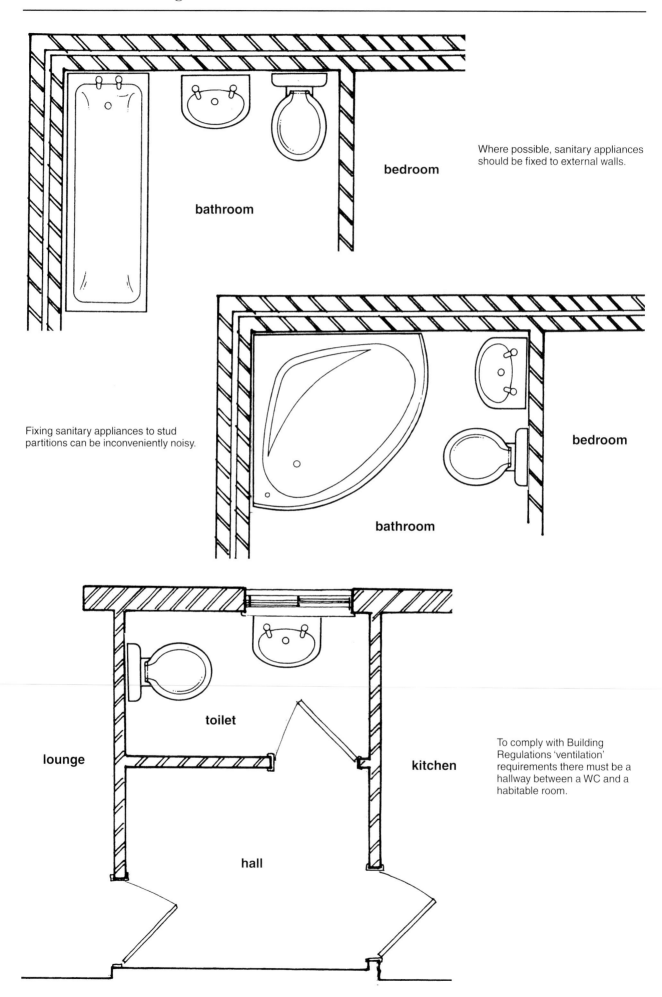

Where possible, sanitary appliances should be fixed to external walls.

bedroom

bathroom

Fixing sanitary appliances to stud partitions can be inconveniently noisy.

bedroom

bathroom

toilet

lounge

kitchen

To comply with Building Regulations 'ventilation' requirements there must be a hallway between a WC and a habitable room.

hall

(Above) The bath panels in limed oak complement the wooden flooring and wainscotting.

(Left) A warm wooden floor covering.

FLOORING

The bathroom is the wettest room in the house so the flooring you use must be suitable for the purpose. You may choose carpets because they can give a feeling of luxury, they are warm to walk on and soft under bare feet. Loose-lay bathroom carpet tiles also may be a good idea because they can be rotated to reduce wear, but whatever you choose it should be quick-drying and easy to keep clean. The synthetic materials from which bathroom carpets are made are specially designed for this purpose. Even around the toilet area, that can be unhygienic, the carpet or carpet tiles should be easy to remove and clean when necessary. Unlike other rooms in the house it will be advisable, when the flooring is laid, to leave it unsecured around the edges for easy removal.

Vinyl flooring is another warm alternative ideal for the bathroom. It is easy to lay and to keep clean and is available in a wide range of colours. Cushioned vinyl is also very good, it is warmer than the non-cushioned vinyl and will also last for many years. If you want to create various designs or just feel that tiles are an easier option to lay, then vinyl tiles are a comparatively inexpensive floor covering and look extremely effective.

Another warm and quiet floor covering is the cork tile. These tiles are very easy to lay but they should be the correct type, with a sealed finish. Wooden strip flooring is becoming very popular in various rooms around the house, including bathrooms. The timber must be sealed to prevent water penetration and must be the type suitable for this wet and steamy environment.

Of the harder and colder flooring tiles ceramic floor tiles will be the most popular. They are likely to be the most expensive covering and must be suitable for flooring, with a non-slip finish. The range of colours, shapes and styles available is very extensive but laying them directly onto a wooden floor should be done only after professional advice. Modern bathrooms generally have upgraded chipboard sheets in the bathroom that are treated before being installed. Securing ceramic tiles here should be acceptable if the manufacturers agree but floorboards, where the floor can have an uneven finish, may need a sheet covering before the tiles are laid. And, of course, ceramic tiles are cold to walk on and

is not possible then mechanical ventilation, by way of an electric fan, can be used providing it produces the required air changes per hour. Similarly a new toilet will not be permitted if it opens directly into another habitable room such as a kitchen or lounge. In these instances there must be a hallway or similar dividing section between the two.

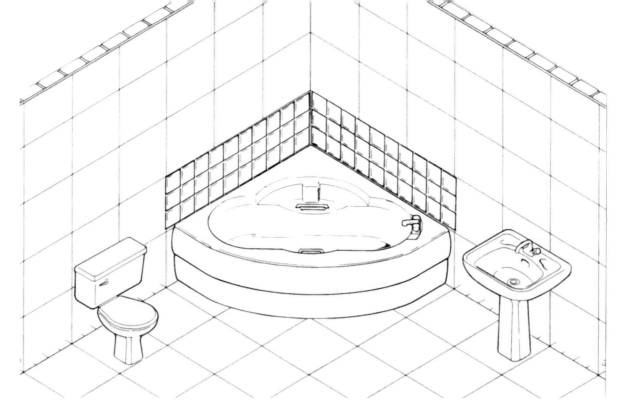

Try to visualize your plan in completion.

will attract some condensation when the bathroom is in use. Smaller carpets laid on the tiles will create the right balance but they should also have a non-slip backing.

WALL TILES

Bathroom walls, like the floors, will have to deal with a higher humidity than any other room in the house. They can be painted with emulsion or gloss paint and they can be papered, but whatever is used must be suitable. Vinyl emulsions and vinyl or washable wallpapers should resist the steamy atmosphere a bathroom creates and are easily available in many colours and patterns. Ceramic wall tiles are also available in a vast range and

are both easy to fit and easy to keep clean. Whether you tile complete walls or just put a splash-back behind the appliances, you can create an extremely decorative effect using contrasting colours and shapes.

Old or existing wall tiles need not be removed provided that they are even and secure but, if they are removed, make sure the new surface is free from loose plaster and the surface is both level and secure.

Imaginative wall tiling can create a bathroom to languish in.

Bathroom Planner Data Sheet (Page 82)

Step by Step
1) Transfer the measurements of your Bathroom area to the grid sheet.
2) For each measurement take more than one reading.
3) Allow for any discrepancies when adding the measurements to the grid.
4) Add the positions of all services (for example, Water, Drainage and Electricity).

Working Areas
1) When considering the new bathroom layout allow enough space for the comfortable use of each appliance.
2) It is quite acceptable for working areas to overlap.
3) Try not to overlap areas where two appliances may be used together – for example, bath and washhand basin.

Electrics
1) The only permitted socket outlet in the Bathroom is a shaver socket.
2) Light fittings, heaters and extractor fans must be operated by pull cord switches that are out of reach of both showers and baths.
3) For safety reasons the light bulbs and fittings must be suitable for bathrooms.
4) Strip lighting or similar will provide good facial lighting behind the washhand basin.
5) Electricity in the Bathroom is a potential killer so discuss any plans you have with a qualified electrician before commencing work.

BEDROOM PLANNING

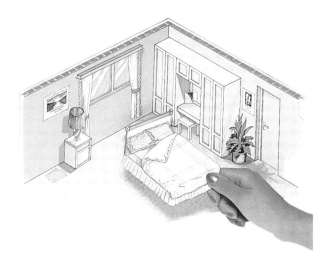

The best way to start the day is to wake up in comfortable and pleasant surroundings. So although you may spend comparatively little time in your bedroom it is worth making sure that the style is a true reflection of your taste and personality and that it is decorated and furnished to provide a relaxing atmosphere.

But a bedroom is not just a room in which to sleep, there are countless other activities to consider with watching television, listening to music and reading all high on the list. Not forgetting, of course, that it may also be a room for intimacy and mood creation or an escape from the everyday grind, but a bedroom should never be considered as insignificant. Estate agents, in their wisdom, may tell you that the kitchen and the bathroom are the important selling points of a house but the first thing any house buyer considers is the number and the size of the bedrooms. On their literature they

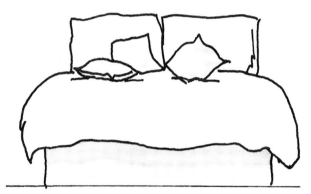

will list first the number of bedrooms a property has and then may well try to sacrifice a reception room such as a dining room or study to list it as another bedroom.

Recognizing how important the bedroom is, and as a bonus to purchasers of new houses, builders, designers and planners are constantly working on the ergonomics of their layouts, trying to maximize what appears to be becoming a smaller floor area. Today the bedroom receives more attention from house designers than any other area of the house, in an effort to reassure their customers that space is not at a premium and to offer up-to-date solutions to relaxation and storage. They know that getting this area well laid out and balanced is extremely important. And they are not alone. Bespoke furniture manufacturers, recognizing that design possibilities are endless and knowing how space and storage occupy a high priority in modern house layout considerations and the minds of prospective purchasers, now offer designer bedrooms alongside their designer kitchens.

(Below) An air of grandeur.

(Above) Cool, Italian-style elegance.

A counterbalanced hanging rail.

Where space is not at a premium a separate dressing room will prove invaluable if you or your partner have a lot of clothes. Or you may even consider partitioning off part of the bedroom to create a narrow dressing room, leaving plenty of wall space for bedroom furniture. Some houses will already have an adjacent dressing room, others will have en-suite facilities and these will all add to the overall ambiance of the property provided, that is, that all the other bedrooms are given similar consideration. Sacrificing a small bedroom to create a dressing room may be practical for personal requirements but could provide a feeling of space shortage to any future prospective purchasers. Always try to use the space wisely and consider all your options. If possible, visit show homes in your area for layout ideas and to keep abreast of changing trends. You may well see the perfect solution to what has become a problem.

As the *bed* is the largest item that the bedroom is going to accommodate, deciding the type and size of the bed, and where to put it, is the first task. For some the luxury of a fully draped four poster will be ideal while others may enjoy the mental and physical relaxation of a waterbed. And if the bedroom is for a youngster or a

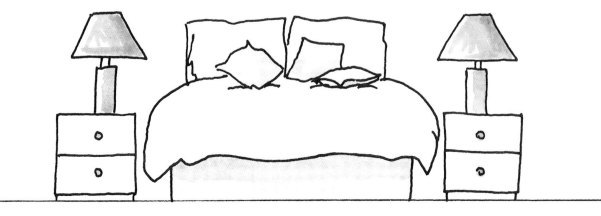

The bed can easily be moved around when you have free-standing bedroom furniture.

teenager then a single bed or even bunk beds may be appropriate. If the bedroom is to be furnished with free-standing furniture then bed positions may be easily changed but if it is to be a 'fitted' bedroom with built-in furniture then deciding the bed position will be very important. Before ordering expensive built-in bedroom furniture, experiment with the bed or beds in various locations just to ensure that all possible considerations have been taken into account.

Where the bedroom is large, furniture can be used to create the style. Chests of drawers, wardrobes and a dressing table will provide storage space for clothing and cosmetics. An ottoman at the base of the bed can be added for extra storage without taking up too much space. The addition of *en-suite* facilities will require more specialized planning but will add another dimension to the master bedroom.

On the other hand, where space is at a premium, built-in wardrobes with a row of high cupboards creating an alcove for the bed is very popular and there are a multitude of designs and manufacturers to choose from. The units may be pre-assembled or flat pack, self-assembly.

Another important bedroom aspect to consider is *lighting*. Natural light from a window or windows will be available in every bedroom with the back-up of general lighting from overhead fittings or from wall and table lamps. Together these will help to create the atmosphere you require. For darker rooms where natural light is at a premium, mirrors and colour schemes can provide additional, reflective lighting when positioned correctly.

Light fittings apart, the other electrical fittings servicing the bedroom will be power points and possibly an aerial socket. If you like to watch television or listen to music the location of these points may also determine

(Above) An organized space frees the mind.

(Left) Make the most of your space.

(Below) Echoing designs of the Edwardian era.

the bed position. On the other hand, you may be a health and fitness follower where room for exercise bicycles or rowing machines may be high on the list of priorities so adequate space must be made available for you to utilize these facilities.

All in all, it is fair to say that the bedroom of the modern home is no longer just a place to sleep. It needs to be multifunctional with careful planning given to storage while catering for a multitude of leisure pursuits and activities.

WHERE TO PUT THE BED

The largest and most conspicuous item of furniture in any bedroom will be the bed. Whether it is a single divan or a four-poster, a master bedroom or a nursery, the bed will be the centre and focus of attention and it will be representative of the style you are trying to

achieve. Of course the room dimensions and layout may dictate where the bed is to be placed, but it is likely that there will be several options available.

The most important factor to consider, at this early planning stage, is 'How long will the bed stay in this location?' If the answer is 'not very long' then the furniture in the bedroom must be free-standing and moveable. On the other hand, if the bed is to remain in the same position 'ad infinitum' then the bedroom furniture can be free-standing or built-in, as required.

Selecting the best bed 'position', therefore, will be key to any furniture plans and the 'position' is likely to depend on three critical points. The first point is 'natural

(Right) Easy to install, sliding wardrobe doors can be very effective.

(Below) Make the most of your space with sliding wardrobe doors.

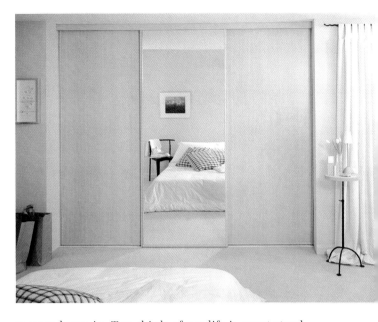

light'. When planning a master bedroom, situating the bed fairly close to a window will allow the natural light to create its own moods and images, unlikely to be achieved when the bed is placed in a dark corner. On the other hand, if you are planning a children's room there will be safety factors to consider as far as windows are concerned.

The second important point to consider is 'access' and this point will be relevant for all bedrooms. The bedroom door location will have a huge bearing on both privacy and how effectively the bed position will work before and after it is in use. Getting in, and out of, bed and dressing should, if possible, be shielded by the opening door. Another point to allow for is making the bed. This can be very awkward when the bed is placed behind or too close to the bedroom door.

And the third most important point to consider is where the bedroom is situated relevant to 'adjacent' rooms. Locating beds back to back with just a bedroom wall to divide them is unlikely to provide the personal seclusion expected from a bedroom.

With these three very important thoughts in mind positioning the bed should be fairly straightforward. So, in short, the bed should be positioned within the light range of the window, not be too close to the bedroom door and, if possible, not back onto an adjacent bedroom wall.

WHAT BED?

Our bed is probably the most underrated piece of furniture we have in the house yet it is the one place we feel most at home in. Two-thirds of our life is spent standing up, sitting down or being on the move, but the remaining third is spent lying down where proper support is essential. A good night's sleep in a warm bed, your own bed, can be so rewarding. Visiting friends or staying in hotels may be great fun but we all look forward to getting into 'our own bed'. The lounge suite doesn't have the same appeal and nor do the carpets yet we spend more money and time selecting these items than we do on our 'nest'. The one place we feel safe and secure, and in fact it is even the place we would all like to die, our own bed. It sounds so natural. And of course our bed is no longer just a place for sleeping in. We may want to watch television, listen to music or read a book, activities not necessarily carried out that easily lying down. So you can see why bed selection is so important and how dramatic a role it plays in our everyday lives.

When you choose a new bed there are three important points you must consider. The first is size. Make sure the bed you choose is large enough for the occupant or occupants using it. If it is too small you will find yourself sleeping diagonally across the bed and feeling generally uncomfortable. Beds are available in a range of sizes starting with single beds, approximately 3ft by 6ft 3in. Double beds are approximately 4ft 6in by 6ft 3in. Queen-sized beds are approximately 5ft by 6ft 6in and king-sized beds are approximately 6ft by 6ft 6in. And if you need something larger, then custom-built beds can be made to your own personal requirements.

The second important point when choosing a bed is support. Buying a bed by its appearance can be a costly mistake. Always lie on it, you may feel slightly embarrassed but it is the most natural thing to do and, in fact, the salesperson will actually expect you to do this. If you have a partner take them along too and both lie on the bed together. Check to see if it really is comfortable, that it is not too soft or too firm. If your partner is a different size, check how this affects the balance or movement of the mattress. It is important to find out now as it may be too late when you get the bed home.

And the third most important point to consider is the type of bed you want. You may both simply view a bed as the place in which you end the day quite happy with just a good night's sleep. For the infirm and for those who suffer from allergies an orthopedic bed or a waterbed may be a consideration. And of course, as I mentioned before, you may use the bed as a place for other activities such as watching television and reading in which case an adjustable bed might be ideal. Whatever bed you eventually choose, and the range is

The flexibility and quality. A fully counterbalanced wall bed.

Three beds in one. A great idea for the growing family.

More than just a bed. The sofa bunk.

enormous, get the best you can possibly afford and make sure you consider who is to sleep in it and what its functions are.

WATER BEDS

Mention a waterbed to a friend or associate and you are sure to get a knowing wink and a wry smile such are the preconceptions about these, so far, underrated beds. Comments like 'Don't you feel seasick?' or 'Aren't they just a bag filled with water?' and 'They must be unbelievably heavy and likely to flood or crash through the floor' are among the standard questions when waterbeds are the topic of conversation. Well, the British Waterbed Association has heard these comments and many more besides, many times, so, for anyone considering a waterbed, they have produced an array of literature to help in the decision-making process. In their literature they discuss what benefits can be obtained from a waterbed for sufferers of short-term and long-term infirmities such as backache and arthritis. They consider how the lack of a 'conventional' spring or foam-filled mattress can be of benefit to asthma and allergy sufferers

The Goldilocks bedroom.

and they also dispel the rumours about how unsafe and unstable waterbeds may be.

According to surveys more money is spent annually on sleep-inducing remedies than is spent on new beds, so it is important that every possible effort is made to ensure that our bed selection is the correct one.

ELECTRICS

Bedroom electrical planning has progressed a great deal in recent years in modern home design. In the past electrical considerations had all too often been simply a couple of well-placed power points and a central overhead light pendant. But thankfully the modern home designers are changing their attitudes and a great deal more care is taken when planning this vital function. And it is important that this service is given the highest priority when you are planning a new bedroom from scratch. The inclusion of cables and light fittings must come before decorating and not after. Today a television can be found in many bedrooms, both for adults and children, so television aerial points should be added to the list. Where to position the light fittings and what fittings to use can be

tricky but these decisions should be made at the earliest possible moment, and are second only in importance to where the bed is to be positioned. Bedrooms do not have the strict regulations of bathrooms or kitchens but with electricity the greatest care must always be taken. Adding power points to the ring main or light fittings to the existing lighting circuit may seem relatively straightforward but it is always advisable to check with the qualified professionals before the work is started just to make sure your plans are feasible and safe.

LIGHTING

The overall lighting considerations in the bedroom will depend entirely upon its occupants. For couples the lighting may need to be both bright and practical, for reading, putting on make-up and dressing, and mood-creating for feeling relaxed and romantic. Brighter lighting around a dressing table should be arranged evenly to avoid casting shadows and direct lighting at the bedside for reading can be accompanied by softer sources of lighting. Overhead lighting operated from a dimmer switch can be mood-creating, so can up-lighters and

Lamps and shades should complement the bedroom style.

Bedside lamps should be directed onto the pillow for reading without dazzling your partner.

well-selected lamp shades. In a teenager's room the lighting for study areas may need to be motivational while in the nursery a warm relaxing background lighting will help to create the perfect 'nest' scenario. You may want to highlight objects or pictures or you may simply wish to reflect the light off the ceiling creating a shadowless softness. And once you start thinking about lighting, remember the bulb. Light fittings alone do not create the mood. For light without glare and to create a cosy atmosphere, Phillips 'softone' will be ideal and for natural, perfect light then Phillips 'halotone' provides a bright, natural halogen suitable for around mirrors and for shaving.

PLUMBING

Water, along with electricity, is one of the two main services likely to be found in the modern bedroom and it is vitally important that both are positioned correctly and work efficiently. Radiators situated beneath windows are there to provide the best possible effect and help to reduce heat loss and should remain there for these reasons. Other radiators, in less critical locations, can be relocated but it is always wise to check with a qualified plumber before taking any irrevocable action. There may not be an obvious reason why a radiator is placed in this position until you try to move it. The same goes when adding a new radiator. A plumber will advise you about both suitable and sensible positioning and whether your existing boiler is capable of dealing with this addition. Any alterations you decide to make should be completed well before the decorating process just in case the outcome is not exactly what you expected.

EN-SUITE FACILITIES

Adding an en-suite facility to a bedroom will require careful planning and expert advice. In some cases the Local Authority Building Inspector may need to be

Make your bedroom cosy and relaxing by using sidelights.

(Above) A stylish mirror/radiator.

(Left) Stylish bathroom furniture.

informed and Building Regulations approval sought. But generally an en-suite facility is simply an addition to the existing system and will not need approval, as such. But, although adding a radiator may be considered an ideal project for a DIY enthusiast, adding a new bathroom is really a job for the professionals.

The two most important points to consider are where will the hot and cold water will come from? And where will the drainage discharge? The easiest solution would be to back an en-suite facility up against an existing bathroom wall but this may not always be possible, and quite extensive planning may be required for the facility to work properly. And if, for example, a new drainage system is required then Building Regulations approval will

be required. The popularity of second bathrooms has had a major effect on manufacturers and many now produce fittings for almost any eventuality and to fit into the very smallest of spaces. Free-standing vanity units are also available where room is limited or even as another addition to assist the smooth running of a busy household.

CUSTOM-BUILT OR OFF THE PEG?

The design of bedroom furniture has improved dramatically over the past 40 years or so. No longer does a bedroom consist solely of a bed, a wardrobe and a chest of drawers. Beautifully designed and manufactured units work together to create an individual living area that reflects our personalities and style. Modern fitted furniture can be designed to personal requirements, provide maximum storage space and yet be adapted to fit any shaped room.

The fully fitted bedroom, installed by professionals, can create the room of your dreams while the range of free-standing furniture is now becoming so extensive, moveable and interchangeable that the options available may better suit the bedroom you are planning.

(Above) A free-standing wash station.

(Right) En-suite with shower in corner location

(Below) En-suite bathroom.

(Below right) A breakfast tray.

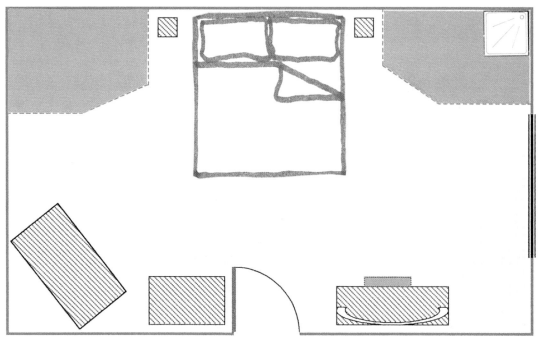

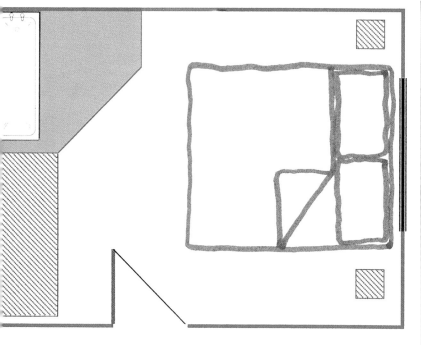

(Above) Indulge in the luxury you deserve.

(Left) A concealed TV unit.

A concealed linen bin.

A master bedroom where the investment in purpose-built, bespoke-designed units will not only be a long term investment but add to the property value should be considered on its own merits. A growing teenager's room, on the other hand, may need changing several times, so long-term investment should be looked at much more carefully and with a certain degree of caution. Where the bedroom occupation is likely to be fixed then plan accordingly and likewise, where the bedroom occupation may include friends staying or room for growth then good planning is important.

Packed with storage potential.

Bedroom units are available, like kitchen units, in flat-pack self-assembly formats and also purpose-built. The decisions to be made must include the life expectancy of this addition and what is its investment potential.

STORAGE

Space has always been at a premium in the modern home and nowhere more so than in the bedrooms. Making room for four bedrooms where only room for three exists has become an art form for some house builders and this puts added pressure on storage space. And of course our own personal wardrobes are far better stocked than those of our parents, so the 'space' problem can become very acute. For this reason bedroom manufacturers are pleased to promote any possible storage benefit to be gained from their own furniture and how best it fits into the space you have. It is true that built-in furniture is the best space-saving design but of course built-in furniture can seldom be moved around when circumstances or requirements change. Where room is at an absolute premium, de-mountable beds and wall-beds could be considered. This is another field where modern advances have greatly improved availability and suitability. Whatever you choose, and the possibilities are almost endless, take your time and make sure the furniture you select suits your bed selection.

THE CHILDREN'S ROOM

The marked difference between an adult's room and a child's room is the room required for growing. An adult bedroom can remain the same for a number of years while a nursery will soon become a child's room then a teenager's room incorporating several decorating processes and furniture changes. A nursery will probably only require a cot, a small storage area and a place to wash and change the baby. Then as years begin to pass the cot will be replaced with a bed and the walls, once pretty and 'twee' may see the addition of wallpaper showing, perhaps, a favourite cartoon character with curtains and bedding to match and the storage areas will expand. Then, in no time at all, the walls will be covered with posters of pop stars and the play areas and bookshelves will be replaced by sound systems and a television.

So bedroom planning for youngsters should be flexible. Where possible the wall coverings should be non-permanent and the lighting easily adaptable. The floor covering is also important and, however young the children, should be soundproof, durable and warm.

And of course the most important point to concentrate on when planning a child's bedroom is safety. Young babies may not be all that mobile in the early months but they are still quite capable of reaching out and touching a hot radiator. Young children, in no time at all, will be dragging chairs across rooms to switch on lights and then there are the windows, these have always been a temptation. There are many ways of avoiding accidents and these are mostly based on common sense. Light switches can be made accessible to children of a certain age but light fittings should be kept out of reach, for example, try not to put a bed directly below a hanging light fitting. Power points should be fitted with special plug covers to prevent tiny fingers or objects being forced into them. And windows should be usable but fitted with appropriate safety devices according to the age of the child.

Most children enjoy having a room of their own. It is somewhere to bring friends, and somewhere to study and somewhere that can easily be changed to match their age and sophistication. Proved that all the proper safety measures are observed then a young child's room should bring joy to both the child and the parent.

OPPOSITE PAGE
(Top) Subtle, symmetrical panelling.
The Neo-Classic design.

(Bottom) A child-friendly, highly practical
bedroom range.

THIS PAGE
(Top) The Tom Thumb bedroom.

(Right) A Goldilocks starter bed.

(Below) Quality cabinet-making at its
best.

Bedroom Planner Data
Sheet (Page 87)

Step by Step
1) Transfer the measurements of your
   Bedroom area to the grid sheet.
2) For each measurement take more than one
   reading.
3) Allow for any discrepancies when adding
   the measurements to the grid.
4) Add the positions of all services (for
   example, Water, Drainage and Electricity).
5) Mark the position of projections such as
   chimney breasts.

Helpful Hints
1) Valuable storage space can be lost by not
   using the space above the bed.
2) Install lights around a mirror in a way not to
   cast shadows.
3) When the bed position is likely to be
   changed use bedroom furniture that can
   easily be moved around.

KITCHEN PLANNER

Measure wall and floor positions.

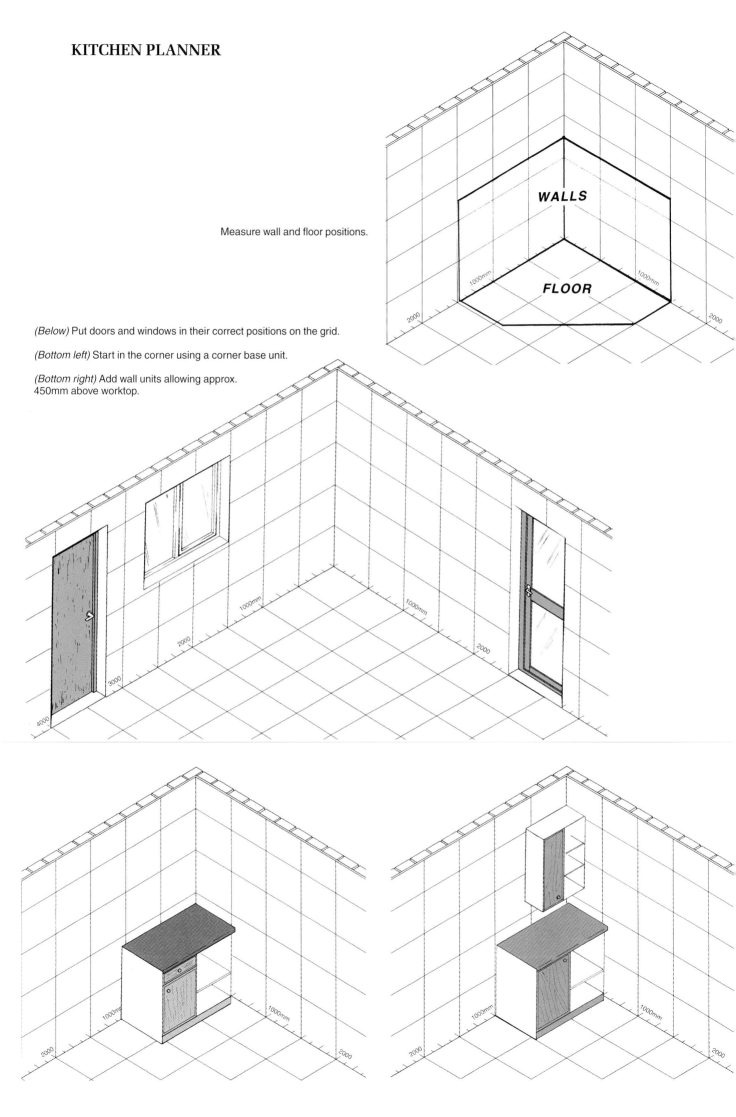

WALLS

FLOOR

(Below) Put doors and windows in their correct positions on the grid.

(Bottom left) Start in the corner using a corner base unit.

(Bottom right) Add wall units allowing approx. 450mm above worktop.

KITCHEN PLANNER GRID SHEET

↑ TOP

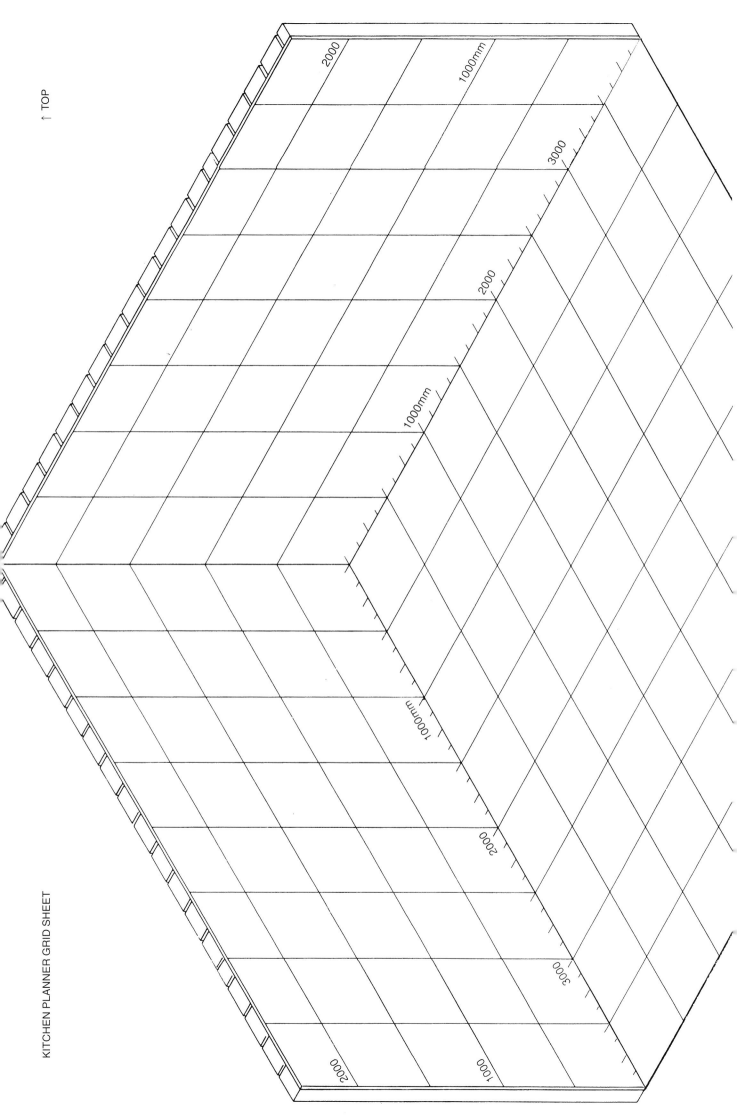

2000

1000mm

3000

2000

1000mm

1000mm

2000

3000

2000

1000

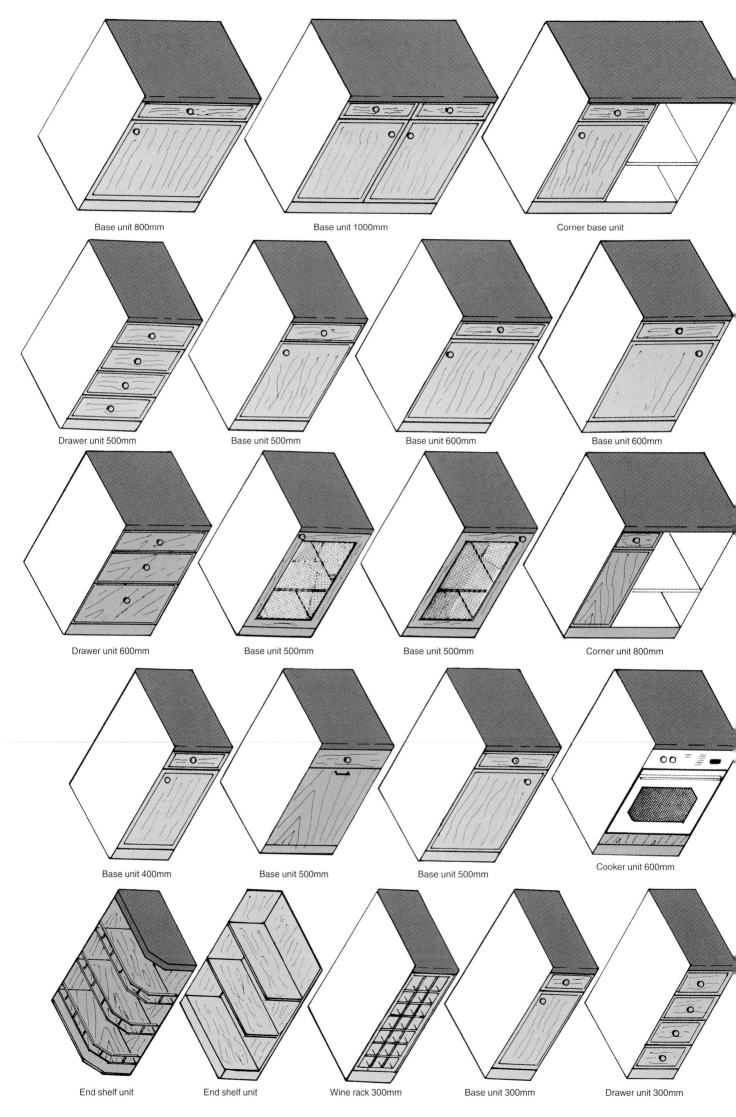

Base unit 800mm

Base unit 1000mm

Corner base unit

Drawer unit 500mm

Base unit 500mm

Base unit 600mm

Base unit 600mm

Drawer unit 600mm

Base unit 500mm

Base unit 500mm

Corner unit 800mm

Base unit 400mm

Base unit 500mm

Base unit 500mm

Cooker unit 600mm

End shelf unit

End shelf unit

Wine rack 300mm

Base unit 300mm

Drawer unit 300mm

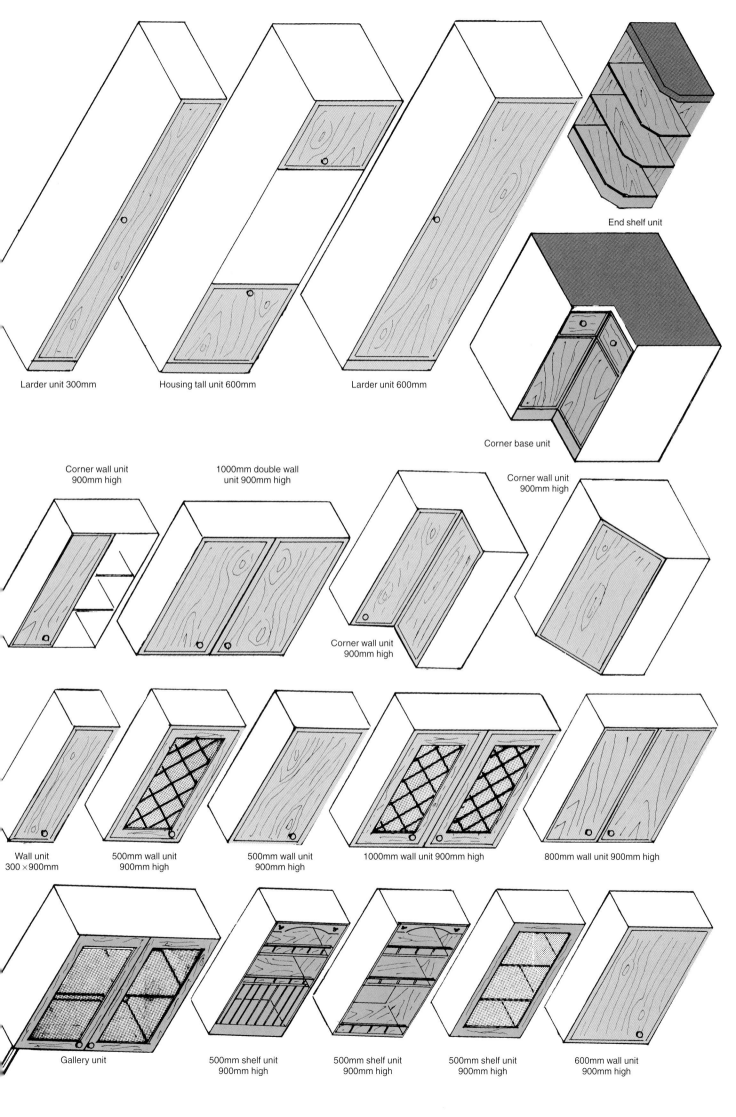

Larder unit 300mm

Housing tall unit 600mm

Larder unit 600mm

End shelf unit

Corner base unit

Corner wall unit
900mm high

1000mm double wall
unit 900mm high

Corner wall unit
900mm high

Corner wall unit
900mm high

Wall unit
300 × 900mm

500mm wall unit
900mm high

500mm wall unit
900mm high

1000mm wall unit 900mm high

800mm wall unit 900mm high

Gallery unit

500mm shelf unit
900mm high

500mm shelf unit
900mm high

500mm shelf unit
900mm high

600mm wall unit
900mm high

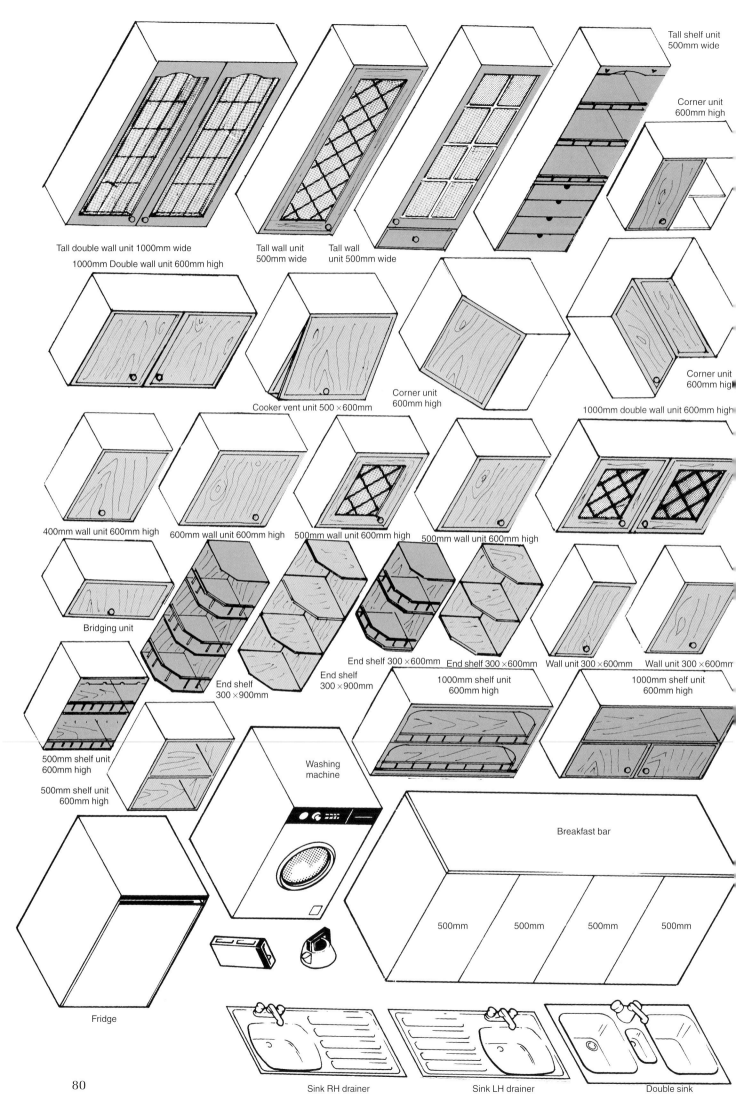

Tall double wall unit 1000mm wide

1000mm Double wall unit 600mm high

Tall wall unit 500mm wide

Tall wall unit 500mm wide

Tall shelf unit 500mm wide

Corner unit 600mm high

Cooker vent unit 500×600mm

Corner unit 600mm high

Corner unit 600mm high

1000mm double wall unit 600mm high

400mm wall unit 600mm high

600mm wall unit 600mm high

500mm wall unit 600mm high

500mm wall unit 600mm high

Bridging unit

End shelf 300×900mm

End shelf 300×900mm

End shelf 300×600mm

End shelf 300×600mm

Wall unit 300×600mm

Wall unit 300×600mm

1000mm shelf unit 600mm high

1000mm shelf unit 600mm high

500mm shelf unit 600mm high

500mm shelf unit 600mm high

Washing machine

Breakfast bar

500mm

500mm

500mm

500mm

Fridge

Sink RH drainer

Sink LH drainer

Double sink

80

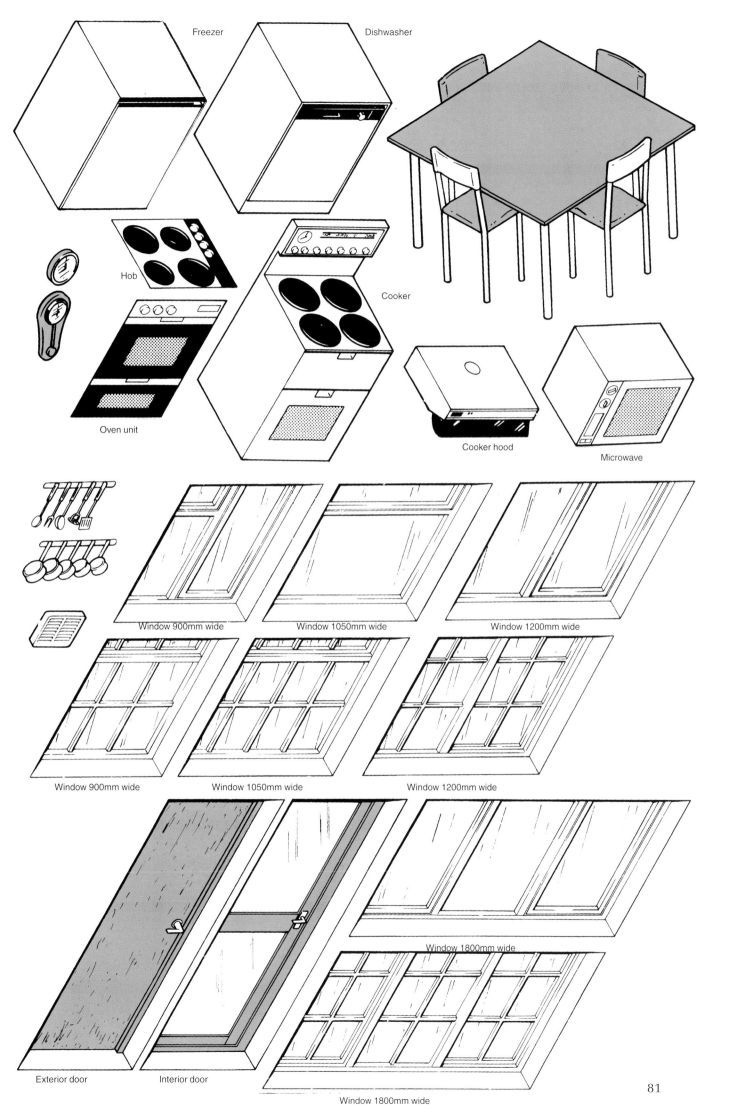

Freezer

Dishwasher

Hob

Cooker

Oven unit

Cooker hood

Microwave

Window 900mm wide

Window 1050mm wide

Window 1200mm wide

Window 900mm wide

Window 1050mm wide

Window 1200mm wide

Window 1800mm wide

Exterior door

Interior door

Window 1800mm wide

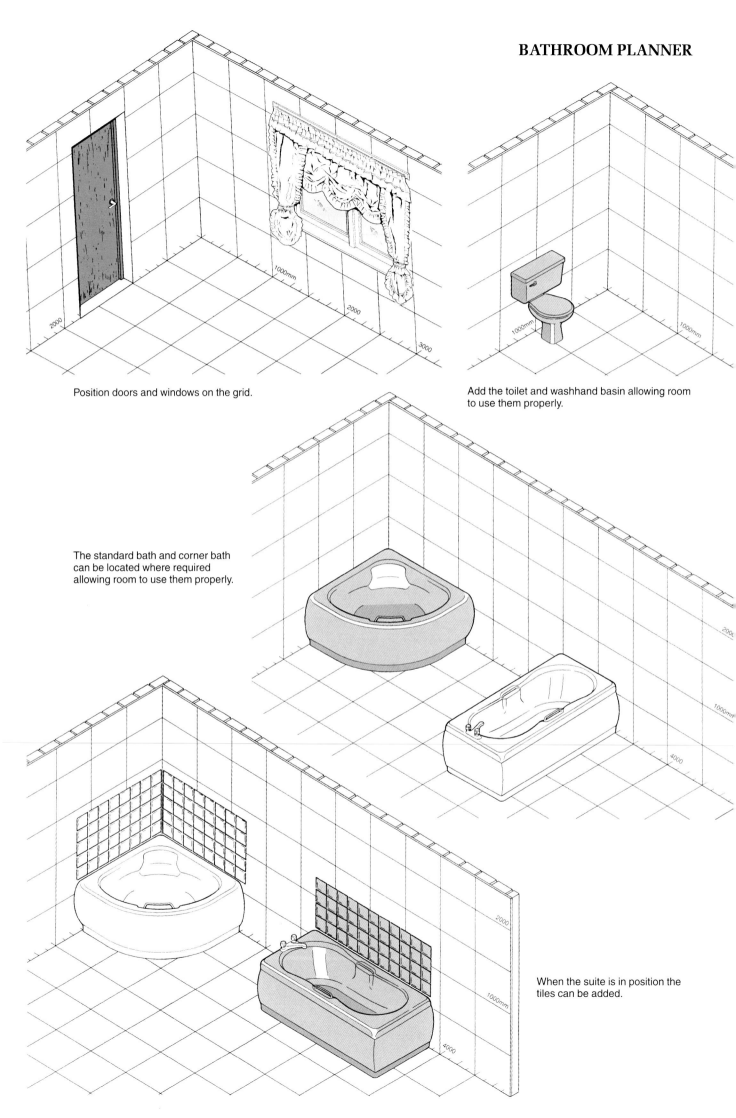

BATHROOM PLANNER

Position doors and windows on the grid.

Add the toilet and washhand basin allowing room to use them properly.

The standard bath and corner bath can be located where required allowing room to use them properly.

When the suite is in position the tiles can be added.

BATHROOM PLANNER GRID SHEET

↑ TOP

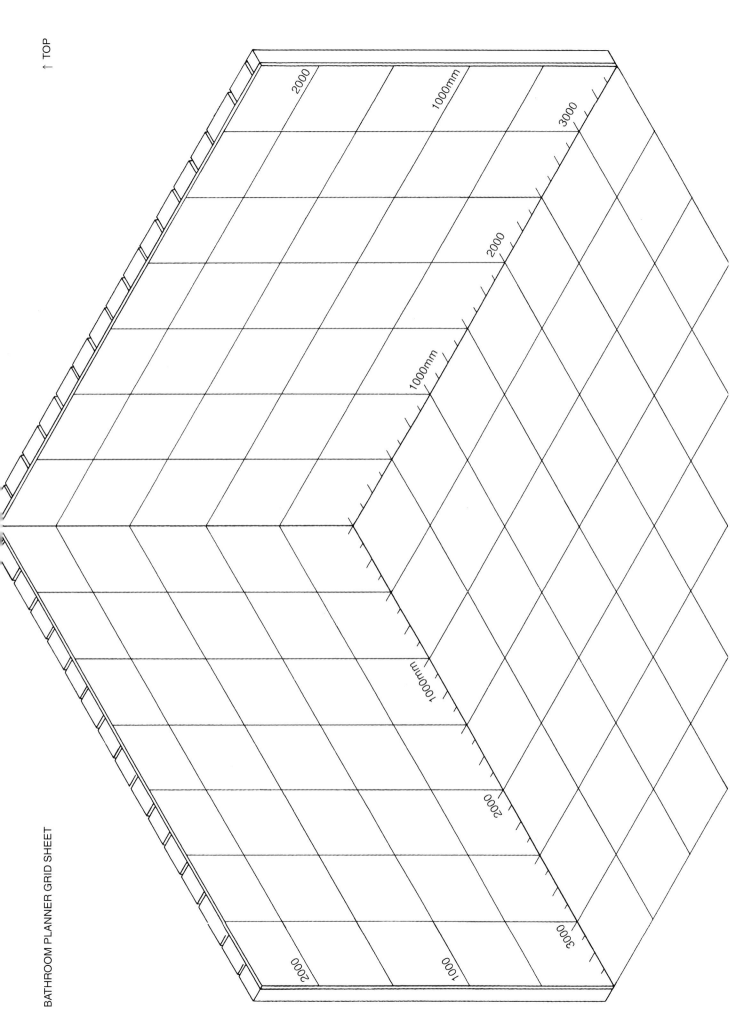

83

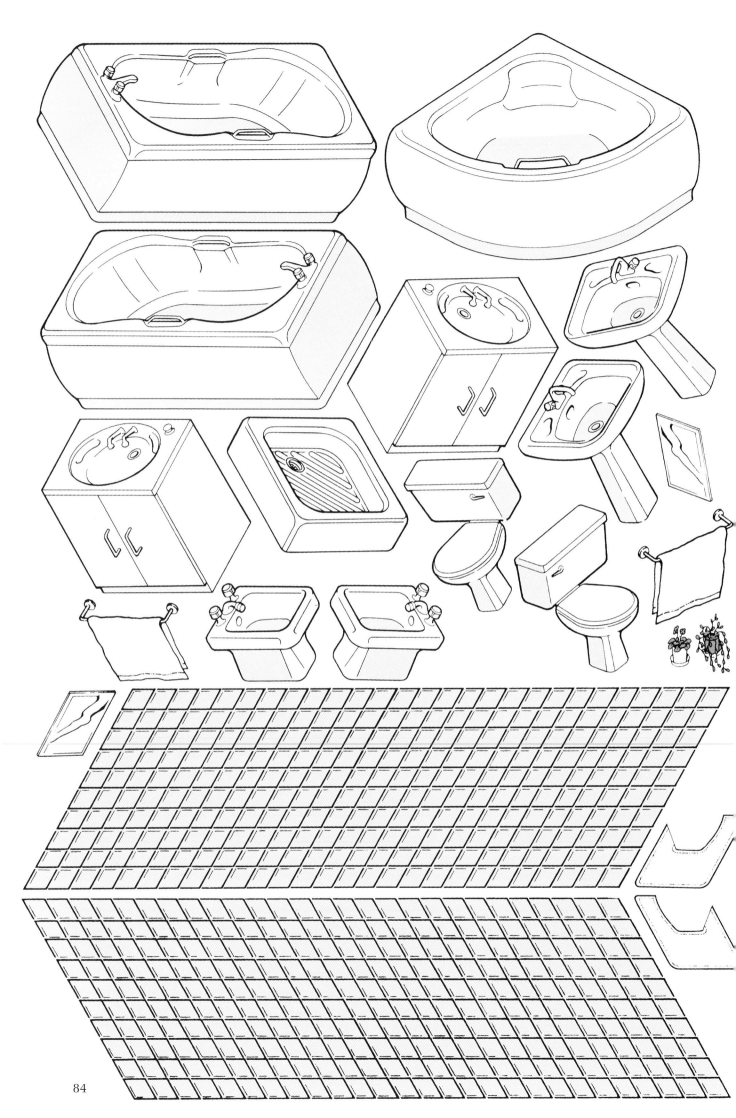

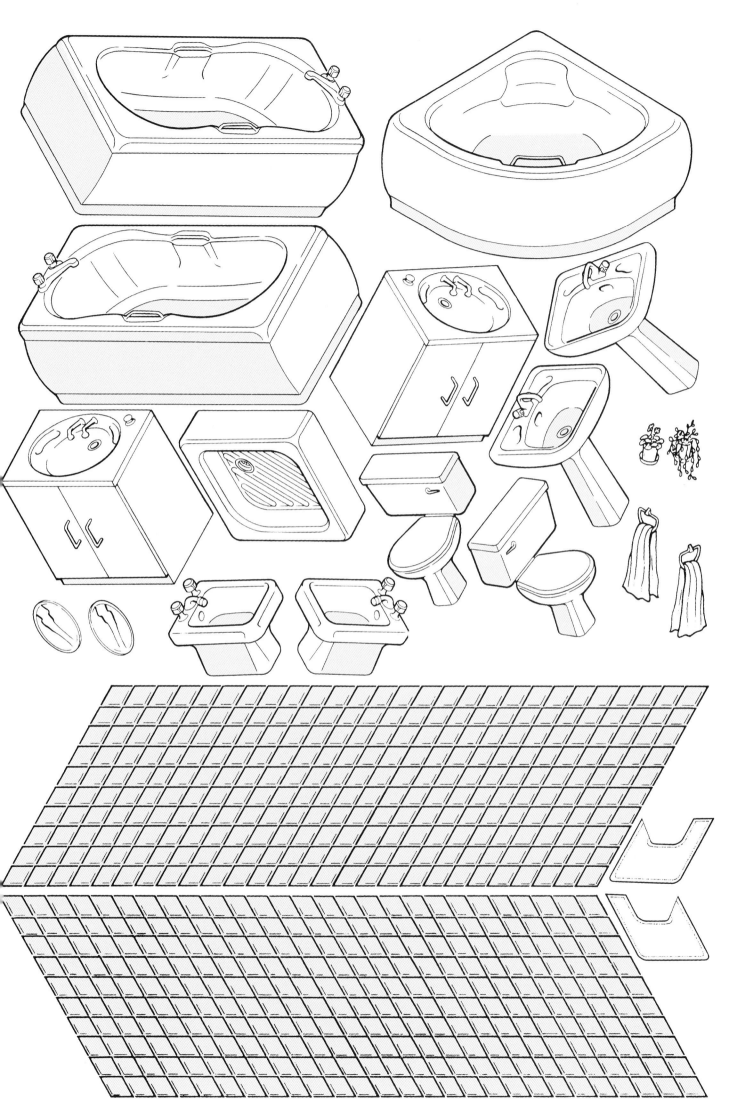

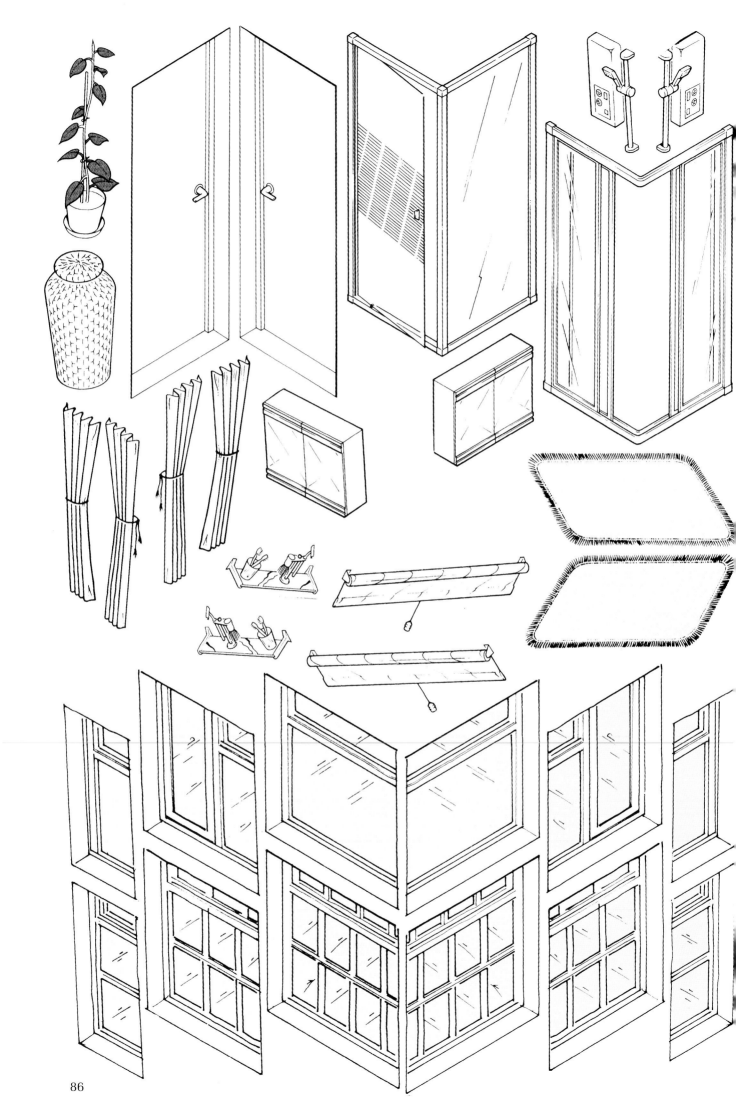

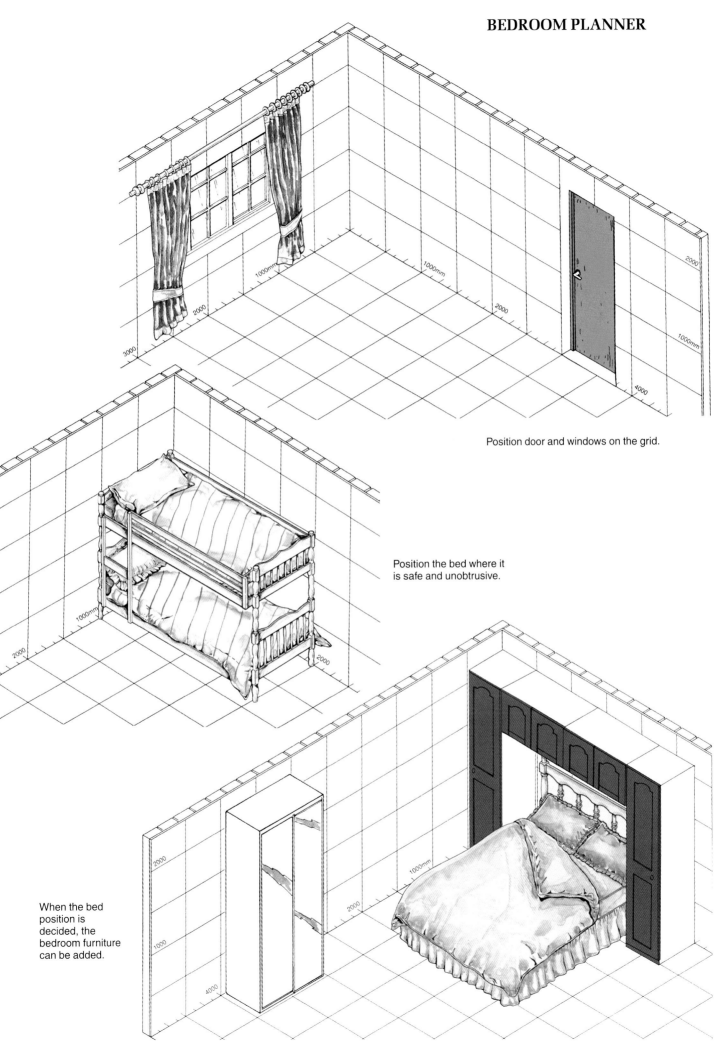

BEDROOM PLANNER

Position door and windows on the grid.

Position the bed where it is safe and unobtrusive.

When the bed position is decided, the bedroom furniture can be added.

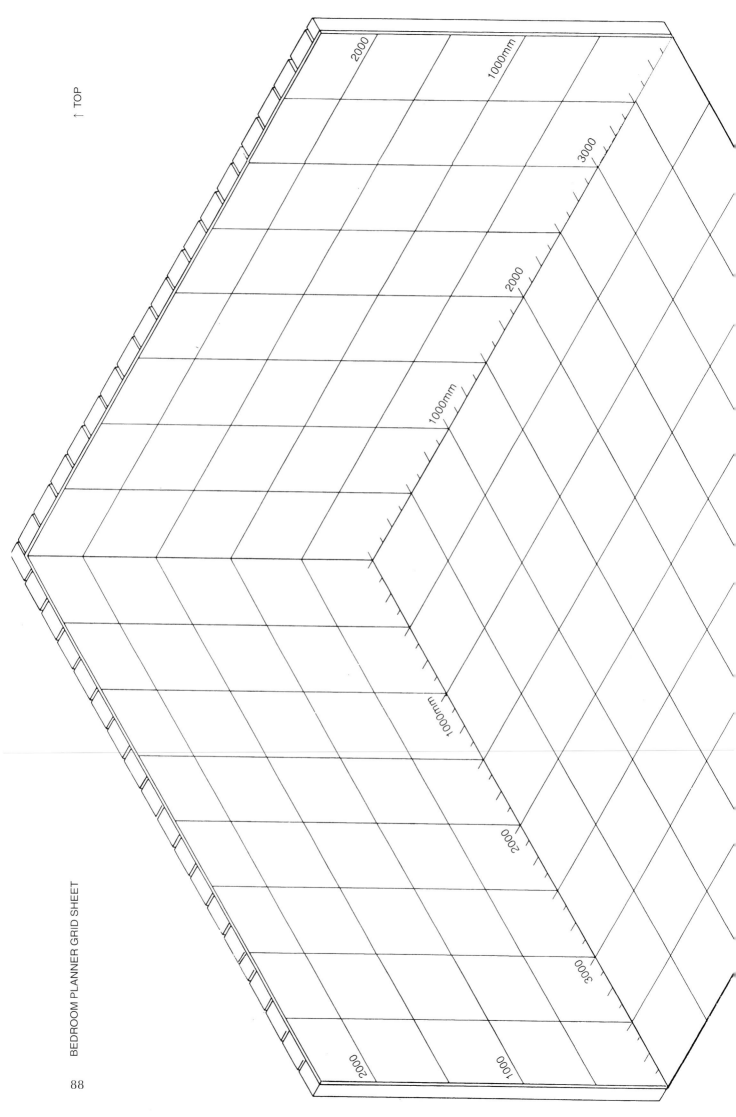

BEDROOM PLANNER GRID SHEET

2000

1000mm

3000

2000

1000mm

1000mm

2000

3000

2000

1000

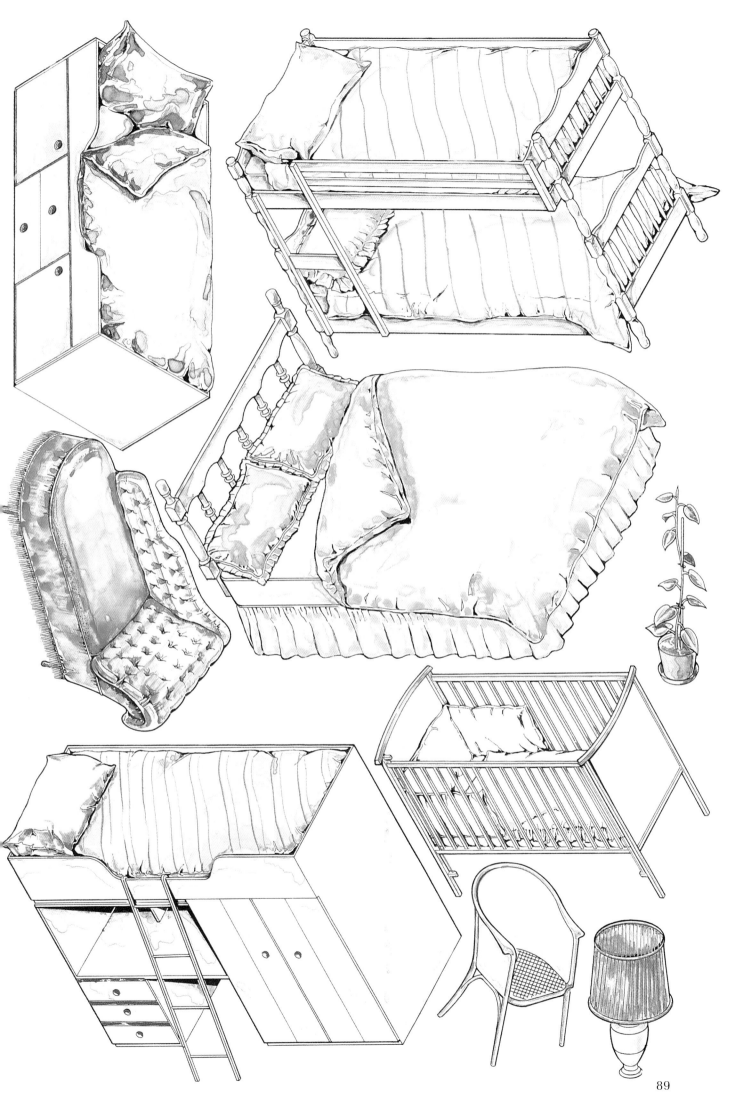

89

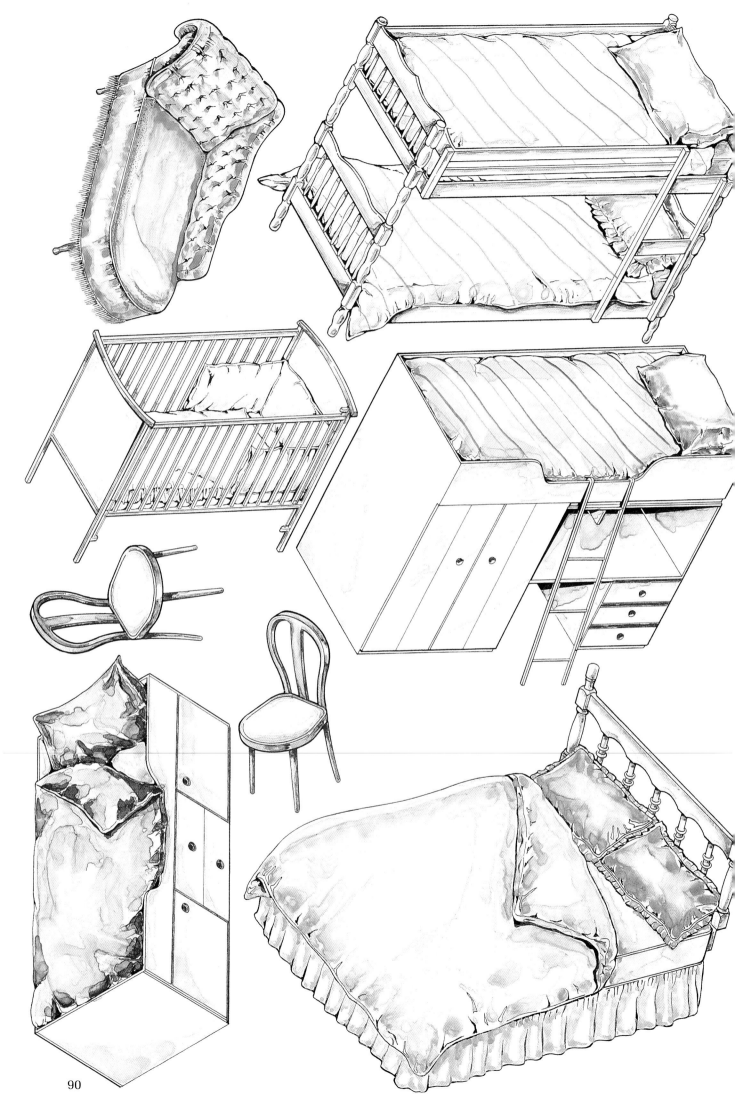

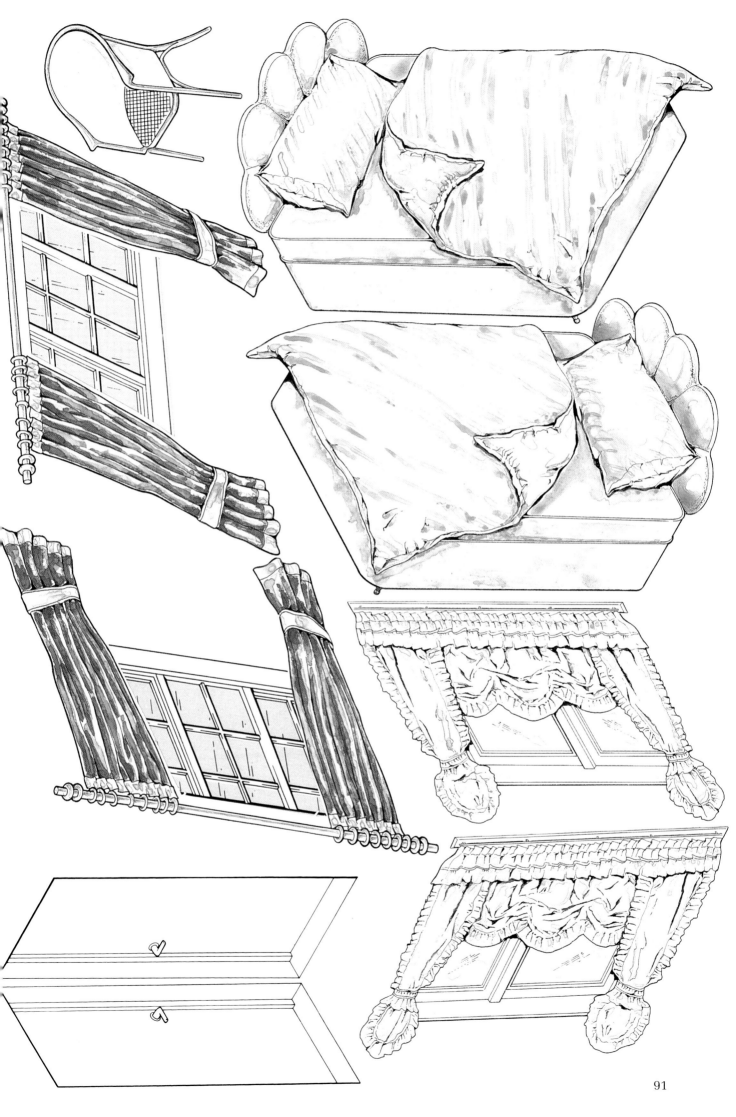

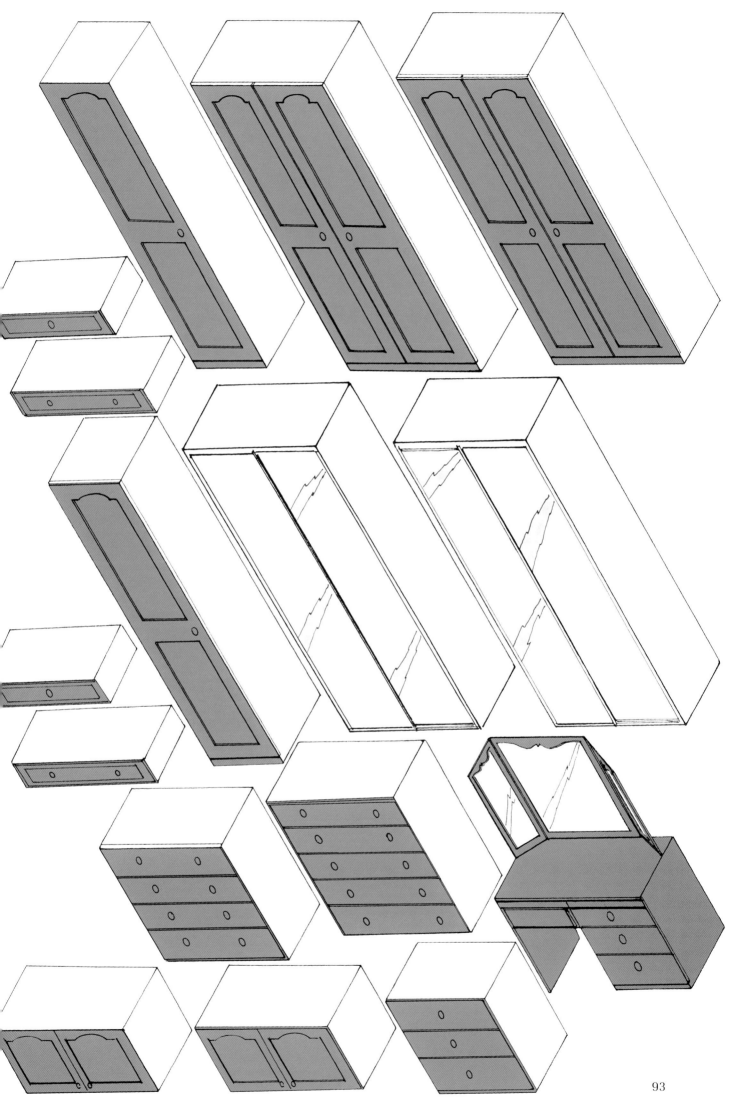

93

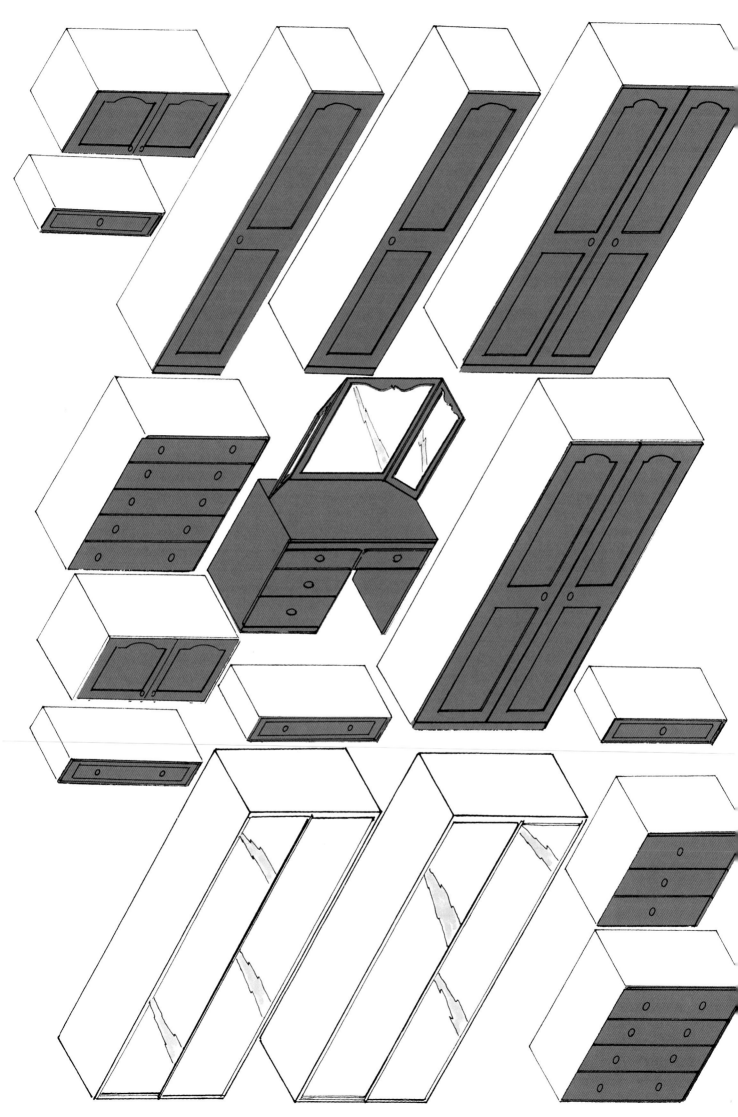

LIST OF SUPPLIERS

Acova Radiators Ltd
Unit E2, Spennells Trading Estate
Spennells Valley Road, Kidderminster DT10 1XS
www.acova.co.uk

B&Q plc
Portswood House, 1 Hampshire Corp. Park
Chandlers Ford, Eastleigh, Hants SO53 3YX

Bordercraft
Old Forge, Peterchurch
Herefordshire HR2 0SD
www.bordercraft.co.uk

British Waterbed Co.
228 Withycombe Village Road
Exmouth, Devon EX8 3BD
www.waterbed.co.uk

Cotteswood Kitchens Ltd
Station Road, Chipping Norton
Oxfordshire OX7 5XN
www.cotteswood.co.uk

Daryl
Alfred Road, Wallasey
Wirral CH44 7HY
www.daryl-showers.co.uk

Doulton Bathroom Products
Cromwell Road, Cheltenham
Glos GL52 5EP

Electrolux Home Products
55–77 High Street, Slough
Berkshire SL1 1DZ
www.electrolux.co.uk

Hammonds Furniture Ltd
Fleming Road, Harrowbrook Ind. Estate
Hinckley, Leicestershire LE10 3DU

Ideal Standard
The Bathroom Works, National Avenue
Kingston upon Hull HU5 4HS
www.ideal-standard.co.uk

Jacuzzi
Silverdale Road,
Newcastle-under-Lyme ST5 6EL

Jay-Be Ltd
Dewsbury Mills, Thornhill Road
Dewsbury, West Yorkshire WF12 9QE
www.jay-be.co.uk

Jewson Ltd
Merchant House, Binley Business Park
Coventry CV3 2TX
www.jewson.co.uk

Magnet Ltd
Royd Ings Avenue, Keighley
West Yorkshire BD21 4BY
For nearest store phone SCOOT 0800 192 192

MFI
For nearest store phone SCOOT 0800 192 192
www.mfi.co.uk

Phillips Lighting Ltd
The Phillips Lighting Centre
420–430 London Road, Croydon CR9 3QR

Shires Bathrooms
Beckside Road, West Yorkshire BD7 2JE
www.shires-bathrooms.co.uk

The London Wallbed Co. Ltd
430 Chiswick High Road
Chiswick, London W4 5TE

Utopia Furniture Ltd
Springvale Business Park, Springvale Avenue
Bilston, Wolverhampton WV14 0QL
www.utopiagroup.com

Visions
Beckside Road, West Yorkshire BD7 2JE
www.visions-bathrooms.co.uk

Wickes Building Supplies Ltd
120–138 Station Road, Harrow
Middlesex HA1 2QB

Mark Wilkinson Furniture
Overton House, High Street
Bromham, SN15 2HA
www.mwf.com

INDEX